Steadfast Self-Hosting
Rapid-Rise Personal Cloud

Adam Monsen

Version 1.2.1, Wed Jun 5 12:17:01 PM PDT 2024: en_US.UTF-8

Steadfast Self-Hosting: Rapid-Rise Personal Cloud

©2024 Adam Monsen. Some rights reserved. This book is licensed under a Creative Commons Attribution-ShareAlike 4.0 International (CC BY-SA 4.0) License [https://creativecommons.org/licenses/by-sa/4.0/].

The beautiful cover art was created by my daughter using Krita [https://krita.org]. You'll find more of her excellent work throughout the book.

Technical editing by Lenny Wondra [https://www.wondra.codes].

First published in 2024 by Sunrise Data Press [https://sunrisedata.io].

Seattle, Washington, USA.

Paperback ISBN: 979-8-9908615-1-0

Library of Congress Control Number: 2024911437

🌈 Sunrise Data Press

Table of Contents

Colophon... ii
Foreword... 1
1. Introduction.. 5
    1.1. Welcome.. 5
    1.2. Supporting the author.................................. 7
    1.3. Book version... 7
    1.4. Copyright and license.................................. 7
    1.5. Disclaimer... 9
    1.6. Style... 10
2. Background.. 13
    2.1. Who am I?... 13
    2.2. Why did I write this book?............................ 14
    2.3. What's with the title?................................ 15
    2.4. Who is this for?...................................... 17
    2.5. What is this book *not*?.............................. 18
    2.6. How write book?....................................... 20
    2.7. A note on FOSS.. 21
3. Your journey.. 23
    3.1. Why you should self-host.............................. 24
    3.2. Why you should not self-host.......................... 27
4. Practical examples.. 29
    4.1. Criminal chickens..................................... 29
    4.2. Photo search by location.............................. 31
    4.3. Surprises... 32
5. Plan.. 37
    5.1. Budget.. 37
    5.2. Resources... 37
    5.3. Schedule.. 38

- 5.4. Transition... 39
- 5.5. Sysadmin mindset............................. 39
- **6. System design**................................... **41**
  - 6.1. Service stack.................................. 41
  - 6.2. Digital security............................... 43
  - 6.3. Filesystem..................................... 48
  - 6.4. Operating system............................ 49
  - 6.5. Contained services.......................... 50
  - 6.6. Reverse Proxy................................ 52
- **7. Implementation**.................................. **55**
  - 7.1. Service plan................................... 55
  - 7.2. Prepare hardware............................ 59
  - 7.3. OS install...................................... 65
  - 7.4. Server maintenance......................... 68
- **8. mario**.. **73**
  - 8.1. mario philosophy............................. 73
  - 8.2. SSH setup..................................... 74
  - 8.3. Provision server.............................. 77
  - 8.4. Server domain name......................... 78
  - 8.5. Start services................................. 81
  - 8.6. Encryption certificates...................... 84
  - 8.7. Tiny test service............................. 85
- **9. Services**.. **87**
  - 9.1. Nextcloud: file sync and share............ 89
  - 9.2. Jellyfin: stream audio and video.......... 91
  - 9.3. Wallabag: save and read articles......... 94
  - 9.4. Watchtower: service updater.............. 96
  - 9.5. Scratch: visual programming.............. 98
- **10. What's next?**.................................... **101**
  - 10.1. Learn more.................................. 101

- 10.2. Use a GPU... 102
- 10.3. AI.. 102
- 10.4. Pi-hole... 103
- 10.5. Single sign-on...................................... 105
- 10.6. Enforce SSH public key auth......................... 105
- 10.7. Allow WAN access.................................... 106
- 10.8. More about Nextcloud................................ 107

11. More resources 125
- 11.1. Support... 125
- 11.2. Alternatives to mario............................... 126

12. Discussion topics..................................... 129

13. Exercises 131

Afterword.. 135

Acknowledgments.. 137

Glossary 139

Index 151

Foreword

Before I started working in open source in 2006, I was working as a community organizer in Massachusetts. I was very well acquainted with how a lack of access to information or not having the "real" instruction manual keeps people from having a say in how they live their lives. As a community organizer, I taught people to lobby. Our organization invited people to work with legislators to draft laws that would address their needs and make their lives better. We taught people to fundraise and we taught them how to organize themselves and their neighbors. And then everything started to move online and important conversations about how we should protect the vulnerable and empower the next generation started happening through our computers.

You can either lament progress or embrace it. I chose to embrace it and decided that I wanted to empower people and help them feel a sense of control over the way they use computers and technology. I started meeting all kinds of people from the free software movement, some were really interested in the way the code worked and others, like Adam, were the most interested in how freely available code could help people.

We met in 2009 at LFNW (LinuxFest Northwest), a free community conference in Bellingham, Washington. A mutual friend had suggested that I should check out Seattle sometime when visiting Washington state for LFNW, which meant carpooling from Seattle to Bellingham. We'd all meet for lunch in Seattle and then do the two hour car ride up to Bellingham together. Those car rides are when we all really started talking about the lack of a free software event in Seattle. We realized we needed some folks in Seattle who could get their companies to sponsor (like Adam and Rob Smith) and someone who could help get some speakers and promote the event to the free software community, which is how I (as a Massachusetts resident) ended up co-founding an annual Seattle event.

Figure 1. Early SeaGL crew. From left to right: Salt, Deb, Patch (with french fry), Adam, Rob. Not pictured: Chris, Jesse, Bri, Lisa, and many more.

SeaGL kicked off in 2013 at Seattle Central College and it was pretty scrappy. No keynotes, lots of shared power strips and a few friends that had gotten roped in to help without a lot of idea of what they'd signed up for. We had chosen a Friday to possibly attract students while the campus was open and a Saturday to make the second day easy for people whose jobs wouldn't support their attendance during the work week. The event was and remains both free to attend and open to everyone.

Adam showed up to our first event with a small pile of "print on demand" hats and shirts with our brand new logo (a seagull of course.)

Talk selection was, "if you want to do a talk, do a talk." Adam gave some great intro talks on Git and Hadoop and I gave a policy talk and community organizing talk. We hadn't written it down yet, but SeaGL was destined to become a conference for beginners and experts, for coders and policy nerds and for talks about the ecosystem; the flaws, the potential and the opportunities for partnership with other efforts to empower people.

After that chaotic first edition, we solidified that we wanted SeaGL to be for everyone, but especially for people who were looking for a way into open source in the diverse, expensive, and tech-heavy Seattle area. We wanted SeaGL to be a great first tech conference for attendees and a welcoming platform for aspiring speakers. We later extended this to working towards finding lesser known speakers and offering them their first keynote opportunity. The whole SeaGL crew (including Adam of course!) have always been passionate about welcoming in newcomers and fastidious about hosting a friendly, safe and curiosity positive environment.

Adam and I have known each other for a long time. I've met his daughter, who is the talented illustrator for this book, and his wife who is also smart and relentlessly curious about how technology affects our lives. I've even met some of the chickens, who are indeed squeaky clean, although sadly not all that smart. Luckily, they are extremely well cared for so they don't need to be too bright.

In brief, Adam is very dedicated to both free software and empowering people. He is also very, very nice! Like truly one of the nicest people I have ever met. If the idea of doing something hard with a patient and gentle mentor is appealing to you and you are curious about self-hosting, then this is the book for you.

Self-hosting is hard. I've personally lurked on mailing lists that were going to make this easy, gone to talks, watched videos and read articles, but they've never quite managed to make it easy. Some of those resources were starting at chapter 2, others were full of comments that made me feel like any random person of reasonable intelligence should be able to find the information that wasn't included. Fortunately, Adam has included everything that a true beginner needs to get started while giving the reader plenty of options.

Self-hosting is also important. Things change quickly in tech and in the wider world. What you control and what you don't is constantly shifting. Self-hosting gives you a chance to keep a few things to yourself and be in charge of your personal data, your media and the way you interact with your computing environment. Self-hosting lets you decide what your needs are and choose how to address them, without asking for permission or getting locked into a contractual relationship with a company that doesn't care about you as an individual.

You should read this book, share it with other people, and maybe, once you're ready, contribute back to the self-hosting community.

Welcome to the world of hosting,

Deb Nicholson

Founder, Seattle GNU/Linux Conference
Executive Director, Python Software Foundation

1. Introduction

Data sovereignty means having full control of your data. It brings the promise of privacy, liberty, and longevity. Realizing data sovereignty is both fun and practical, and supports prosocial behavior. Self-hosting (running your own server) is an excellent path to data sovereignty.

This book will help you efficiently learn and practice self-hosting. You'll gain confidence facing its challenges while enjoying its benefits first-hand. The skills you will build are applicable at home, at work, and in your community.

1.1. Welcome

I am so glad you're here!

I'd like to help you get a server up and running. The self-hosting ecosystem is crowded and confusing, so I've taken care of a number of difficult choices with sensible, tested defaults. I'll help you provision (set up) your own server and a few useful web services. Bring along whatever sysadmin experience you've got, some willing users, and a desire to gain self-hosting competency.

The Internet is often a relentless cash-grab and attention vampire. Our actions are infinitely measured; *we* are the product. The smog of surveillance stifles our freedom and erodes trust. We will:

- Not settle for cheap cloud services.
- Reduce distractions.
- Cherish our attention, time, and freedom.
- Breathe the crisp, clear air of reduced surveillance by providing our own alternative to the chilling popular default of trading privacy for convenience.
- Save money by efficiently running lots of services on our own hardware with negligible incremental cost.
- Do well by our friends, families, and social groups.
- Do things we can't do with public services because we have full access to all our own raw data.
- Adapt and grow as software evolves, taking our data and metadata along with us.
- Share what and when it makes sense to share with whom we trust.

This is the book I wish I'd had when I was struggling to provide a safe online experience for my kids.

New self-hosters can use this book to get started. Experienced self-hosters can compare my choices to theirs.

1.1.1. Prerequisites

To get the most out of this book, the sysadmin experience you bring along should include the ability to configure your router and LAN (local area network), install Linux on a computer (hereafter referred to as your *server*), connect to your server with SSH (secure shell), edit text files and run commands on your server, and transfer files to and from your server.

If you're unfamiliar with any of these concepts, a quick trip to your favorite search engine or local user group should yield enough pointers to get started.

I recommend hosting on bare metal (tangible nearby computer hardware), and this comes with some prerequisites for the physical space where your server resides. Read more about the ins and outs of bare metal in Section 7.2, "Prepare hardware".

Finally, some best practices to keep in mind as you read along:

Document everything you do, if only for your future self. Recruit and train help, leveraging said documentation to share knowledge. Focus, take breaks, be patient, and take care of your body. Ask for help and ask for feedback. Listen to users, gather data, and adapt accordingly.

1.2. Supporting the author

I wrote this book with my own resources after years of research with lots of help from awesome people. See Acknowledgments (near the end of the book).

Please buy a copy [https://selfhostbook.com/buy/] for yourself or someone else, especially if you'd like me to write more books in the future.

1.3. Book version

This book was generated on **Wed Jun 5 12:17:01 PM PDT 2024** with `LANG` set to `en_US.UTF-8` from source `steadfast.asciidoc` at commit `b0eecd5`, branch `main`, tag `1.2.1`, on **Ubuntu 22.04.4 LTS**.

1.4. Copyright and license

Steadfast Self-Hosting: Rapid-Rise Personal Cloud is ©2024 Adam Monsen. Some rights reserved.

1.4.1. Copy this book

This book is licensed under a Creative Commons Attribution-ShareAlike 4.0 International (CC BY-SA 4.0) License.

You are free to...

Share

copy and redistribute the material in any medium or format

Adapt

remix, transform, and build upon the material

The licensor cannot revoke these freedoms as long as you follow the license terms.

Under the following terms...

Attribution

You must give appropriate credit, provide a link to the license, and indicate if changes were made. You may do so in any reasonable manner, but not in any way that suggests the licensor endorses you or your use.

ShareAlike

If you remix, transform, or build upon the material, you must distribute your contributions under the same license as the original.

No additional restrictions

You may not apply legal terms or technological measures that legally restrict others from doing anything the license permits.

Notices

You do not have to comply with the license for elements of the material in the public domain or where your use is permitted by an applicable exception or limitation.

No warranties are given. The license may not give you all of the permissions necessary for your intended use. For example, other rights such as publicity, privacy, or moral rights may limit how you use the material.

1.4.2. Copy this book's code, too

See Chapter 11, *More resources* for how to get the source code. It includes two original works for you to copy, modify, and share. First, the book itself, along with code to generate beautifully typeset versions. Second, a learning tool called mario (see Chapter 8, *mario*).

The license for all original source code related to this book is the GNU AGPL (Affero General Public License) as published by the Free Software Foundation, either version 3 of the License, or (at your option) any later version. A copy of the AGPL is included in `mario/COPYING`.

1.5. Disclaimer

I offer no warranty and no guarantee. Buying or reading this text is not an agreement for support.

While every precaution has been taken in the preparation of this book, I assume no responsibility for errors or omissions or for damages resulting from the use of its code or contents.

I am not professionally affiliated with the products or paid for by the companies mentioned in this book. Their copyrights, trademarks and intellectual property are their own.

My opinions are my own.

I include direct references to many products and companies and add my specific, hard-won lessons on their comparative strengths and weaknesses. My intent is to educate and inform.

I will take shortcuts. I will not seek to deeply and exhaustively explore each topic. I want you to get to the good stuff quickly, then decide if, when, and where you want to dive deeper.

If you find contradictions to these statements, please let me know.

I'm human and error-prone. I'll make it easy to contact me about missing or incorrect information and to improve it yourself if you choose. Please do! See Chapter 11, *More resources* for contact information and how to share improvements.

1.6. Style

Text formatting:

Table 1. Typographical conventions

Styled example	Used for
`zpool status -t`	Inline command, filename, username, password, or variable. Longer snippets of console text use language-specific syntax highlighting.
`Ctrl` + `c`	Key(s) pressed on the keyboard.
example.com	Bare (un-named) link. https scheme is assumed and omitted.
Example domain [https://example.com]	Named link. Full URL appears in print version.
`https://cloud.example.com`	Non-working example link. Replace `.example.com` with your actual domain name.
Chapter 6, *System design*	Cross-reference to another section or chapter.

Admonitions:

 Admonitions like this note draw your attention to auxiliary information.

 Here's a tip,

 something of import,

a cautionary message, and

 a specific warning.

Sidebars:

> Stand-alone or supplemental content may be visually separated using a sidebar like this one. Sidebars may or may not have titles.

Code snippets:

Listing 1. Example code snippet (server)

```
echo foo | sed s/foo/bar/
```

Snippet titles may indicate where the code should be be run. If the location is omitted, one or more intended runtime environments will be explained in context. " server" indicates this particular example Bash script snippet is intended to be run on your server.

2. Background

You might be thinking, "this looks like a lot of background!" And you'd be right.

I go deep into background here because of something I found while giving talks about self-hosting: people know how to learn and discern, they wish for meaningful motivation to commit to learning.

I hope you find that here.

2.1. Who am I?

I'm a dad, tech entrepreneur, and FOSS (free and open source software) enthusiast. I love to parent, care, laugh, sing, listen, code, build, produce, debug, architect, debug, lead, manage, debug some more, lecture, and write. I'm good at administering and securing systems and processes while ensuring privacy, compliance, and reliability.

I'm most proud of my family, growing Mifos [https://mifos.org], founding SeaGL [https://seagl.org], selling C-SATS [https://csats.com], and writing this book.

I've been running my own services for decades. I started with a blog and photo album running on a buddy's machine. The feeling of freedom and control was exciting and it complemented my effectiveness at work, so I kept on, running many of my own services, although rarely on my own hardware.

Once I had a family, our data storage and capability needs increased. A simple network drive and file sync were no longer enough. We were all stuck at home and online at the start of the pandemic, and I was wary of companies swooping in to capitalize on our captivity. I started dabbling more with self-hosting at home and found it suprisingly easy, useful, and fun. I wanted more services for managing our data and I enjoyed the autonomy of our own bare metal.

Around the same time, I decided to de-Google (stop using Google). The family needs and my de-Googling coincided well. Self-hosting was a serendipitous fit. Just *trying* to de-Google was a fascinating and fulfilling journey, punctuated with many self-hosting experiments.

2.2. Why did I write this book?

I wrote this book to promote data sovereignty as a prosocial behavior. This is easier to achieve than ever before with self-hosting, and I wanted to share that in book form. Existing books lack a good, fast, and cheap technique for self-hosting on bare metal. I figured one out and I think you'll love it. It works fine if you run your server in the cloud too, it just costs a lot more (see Section 7.2.1, "Server").

Also, learning is fun. I learn when I write. While learning how my phone works, it struck me how important it is to understand *how "the cloud" works*, since the modern phone experience relies heavily on services and data in public clouds. In trying to make my phone "my own" (do what I want to help me live my best life), I was inspired to host my own data in my own cloud.

Also, most tech folks I know self-host *something*, likely something I've never heard of. There's always another self-hosted service to try out, learn about, improve, and share.

Also, I wanted to write the book I wish *I* had when I started self-hosting.

Also, so there's a *book* about this. There are countless videos, articles, and chunks of code online for doing everything in this book and more. Many are excellent. This book is your to keep, hold, and refer back to as you try, test, and learn.

Also, there's a stark gap between useful individual computers and useful cloud services. It's easy to pay for cloud, but the true price is obscured: surveillance, lock-in, inflexibility.

Also, I can picture a future where owning a truly privacy-respecting home data appliance becomes as commonplace as owning a refrigerator. Creating this appliance has been attempted many times and it'll be attempted again. Until it succeeds and sticks, self-hosting—setting up a server and services for yourself and others—is a great way to go.

2.3. What's with the title?

2.3.1. Steadfast Self-Hosting

I like the word *steadfast*. It reminds me of reliable things and people.

The key to reliable self-hosting is data sovereignty. Software will change, services will change, you will change and the world will change. You've got to have control of your data if you want it to reliably serve you well through all that change.

It does make a difference to have your own copy. You might lose access to something you "bought" because you were actually renting it. It might even change right under your nose. More on this:

- PlayStation To Delete A Ton Of TV Shows Users Already Paid For [https://kotaku.com/sony-ps4-ps5-discovery-mythbusters-tv-1851066164] by Ethan Gach

- What is DRM? [https://defectivebydesign.org/what_is_drm] by the Free Software Foundation

- It's Their Content, You're Just Licensing it [https://nytimes.com/2023/04/04/arts/dahl-christie-stine-kindle-edited.html] by Reggie Ugwu

Saving copies of data someone else is hosting for you is fine. Self-hosting goes a step beyond, giving you far-reaching control of how your data are used and shared. You'll gain agency over authoritative copies of your files, allowing you to know and control your source of truth. All this with reliability and flexibility within a reasonable budget.

Self-hosting means providing computing services by and for individuals, families, and hobbyists in SOHO (small office / home office) environments.

"Small community hosting" is perhaps a more accurate and appropriate term here. You're reading the right book to host services for a small community.

Last, a note on terminology. When it comes to compilers in computer science (and perhaps also other areas in tech), "self-hosting" refers to the wonderfully satisfying milestone when a programming language is able to compile itself. I apologize to my friends in related disciplines for blatantly overloading the term "self-hosting" to mean small community hosting. You had it first, I'm borrowing it and hoping our contextual lane lines will sufficiently prevent collisions.

2.3.2. Rapid-Rise Personal Cloud

Rapid is there to get you excited to jump right in and learn. *Rapid* does not mean *reckless*! I'm a strong advocate of a thoughtful and robust approach to self-hosting. When you encounter a challenge, slow down to learn faster. Once you understand a concept, practice it. Fail fast and often, with rapid iterations trending towards perfection.

Rapid-rise is something you might find on a package of baker's yeast, and I love fresh-baked bread. If your server is a loaf of bread, this book is your rapid-rise yeast.

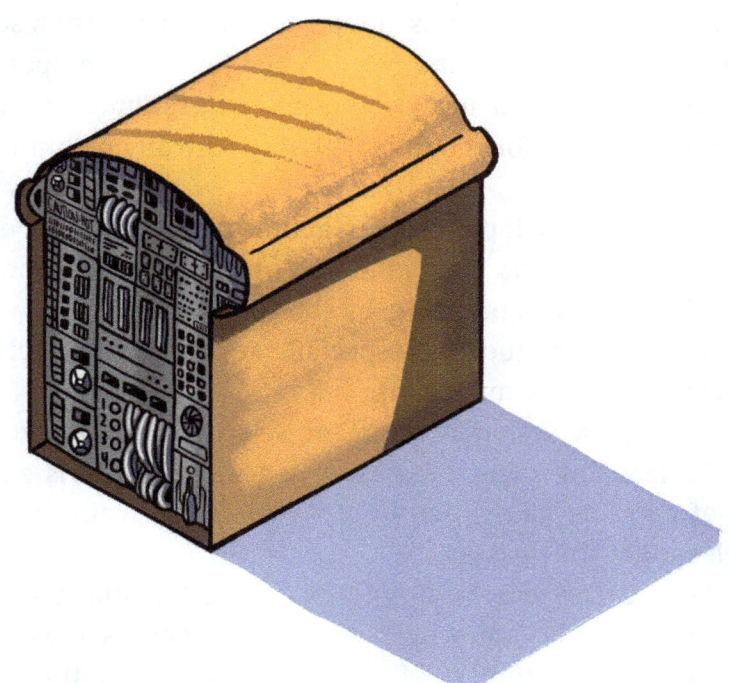

Figure 2. Server in the shape of a loaf of bread.

Cloud implies scalable and automatable. *Personal* scopes that scalability to what's reasonable for a small group. A bare metal server can scale (to a degree) within its box. It can scale automatically by using more or less power according to compute demand, and manually when you upgrade hardware components (say, adding another hard drive).

I'll also admit my inner child enjoys multiple meanings of the phrase *Personal Cloud*.

2.4. Who is this for?

This book is for people who are kind to others, brave in trying new things, curious about the possibilities of self-hosting, and either uncertain how to do so or eager to improve their existing homelab (self-hosting setup).

This book is for people who want to know where their data live, and to be able to work all kinds of magic with it. It's a "from scratch" or "the hard way" approach, and it keeps the doors wide open to many possibilities with a principled self-hosting technique. I'll sometimes recount what worked for me rather than specifically recommend what you should do.

This book is for people curious about or already biased towards FOSS. And—as much as I'll blather on about FOSS—I'm not here to judge. I'm here to *grow*, primarily by sharing and learning.

This book is for students, especially tech-savvy or tech-adjacent students active in clubs and teams.

This book provides motivation for self-hosting with an excellent process for learning same. Its version-specific material is expected to fall out of date. Its motivation and process for learning will become more relevant as time passes.

This book is for those trying to live more for others and less for themselves; selfishly enjoying the act of being selfless. Leaders, parents/guardians, members of a collective or a handful of friends. People who want to self host, who *also* love others and doing other things besides systems administration. I'll save you some precious time for those other things while making the sysadmin bits fun.

Similar to "small community hosting", *Small Group Cloud* would be more accurate title words than *Personal Cloud*. "Small group" is a great target size for what you'll create. I wouldn't bother doing all this just for yourself.

This book is for people into (or hoping to get into) self-hosting. It is geared towards useful, secure, and quick setup of a single bare metal server with many services.

This book is for people who want to *de-Google, de-iTunes, de-OneDrive, de-Dropbox, de-Whatever*.

2.5. What is this book *not*?

This is not a comprehensive guide to self-hosting. I won't attempt to enumerate the endless ways to mix and match hardware, operating systems, isolation techniques, and services. This book is for small scale.

Look elsewhere for:

- high availability
- enterprise security
- N + 1 redundancy
- managing many machines
- clustering
- single sign-on
- advanced monitoring and metrics centralization
- regulatory compliance
- intrusion/threat detection/prevention
- in-depth security hardening
- running your own container registry
- 100% offline / off-the-grid self-hosting

There are some topics like these I'll skip or cover only briefly. Any one of these topics is an entire industry, another piece of hardware, a setting on your home router, a potential career, none or all of the above, and otherwise well worth further consideration. You can and should be aware of them. If you feel I've completely omitted proper detail about something critically relevant to my method of self-hosting, please let me know.

This book is not for the heavily-resourced already-done-thats. If you have $50k and unlimited time to spend on your concrete bunker homelab... well then, may I have a tour? I would *love* to see that. If you are more curious than certain you may still enjoy learning from my choices.

I'm not writing to accommodate hardline software patent and license activists. These wonderful folks will spot my intentional use of the word *open* and omission of the word *libre*. I love all these words, I agree words are important, and I stand on the side of inclusion at the cost of idealism (while maintaining hope these concepts are not mutually exclusive). I thank the activists for helping swing the needle towards freedom, to all our benefit.

This book is not a manifesto for always/only self-hosting. It's fine to self-host some services and pay for others. You'll come up with your own checklist for what to self-host and when. Mine focuses on providing a useful, reliable, future-proof cloud for me and my family.

This book is not the fastest path to trying out web services. You can usually find demo instances running for particular projects. There are cloud providers that will run a service for you and host your data.

See also: Section 11.2, "Alternatives to mario".

2.6. How write book?

Why are you talking like a caveman?

I wrote the book originally in Markdown plain text in my steadfast text editor, Vim [https://www.vim.org]. I applied generous amounts of Pandoc [https://pandoc.org], time, and love. Pandoc is a fantastic FOSS tool which allowed me to use that single plain text file with fairly human-readable Markdown syntax to generate several different decent outputs. While revising, I came across the build system for Pro Git 2 [https://github.com/progit/progit2] (thank you Scott and Ben!). In short order I converted the book to AsciiDoc [https://asciidoc.org] and ported my typesetting code to Asciidoctor [https://asciidoctor.org]. This simplified the book build and gave me more and better output formats.

 Check out the source code—you're welcome to hack away at it. See Chapter 11, *More resources*.

I tried to stick with off-the-shelf FOSS software as much as possible, with minimal customization. This helped me focus on the content while keeping the book simple enough to self-publish.

2.6.1. When write book?

Still with the caveman. Enough already. I wrote this in 2023. And, listen, even blessed cave-dwellers like us should give self-hosting a shot. We got this!

2.6.2. Where?

Seattle.

2.6.3. Hey now.

Admittedly, those last few sections exist so I could cover all 5 Ws [https://en.wikipedia.org/wiki/Five_Ws] and include the caveman gimmick.

2.7. A note on FOSS

I prefer FOSS over non-FOSS. This can be a polarizing topic. Heck, even using the term FOSS instead of the other variants can be polarizing. These are just distractions. Today we need compromise, patience, and kindness. Curiosity over certainty.

Here's my promise to you, dear Reader:

I will try not to get too preachy.

I will prioritize *practical* solutions over *idealistic* ones. I will sometimes fail to do this when it comes to FOSS. Most notably, I will barely acknowledge the existence of non-FOSS alternatives in this book.

I'm aware of the tension between practical and idealistic solutions, and I believe this tension is a Good Thing because it reminds us to think critically about what cloud services we *should* pay for and use, not just what we *can* pay for and use. It's worth a moment's thought.

Our data matter and our personal choices matter. The impact spreads to the groups you are a part of, as does the opportunity for improvement.

I believe self-hosting FOSS is doable and affords many practical benefits over non-FOSS.

Hang in there and give me some feedback. You'll strike your own balance between idealism and practicality and I'm interested to know where you land.

3. Your journey

Continuing advances in hardware and software means self-hosting today is easier and cheaper than ever before. And in one key way, much more complex: there are an overwhelming number of choices to be made for someone starting out on this journey.

Hang in there. I'll help you narrow the choices by providing specific, focused guidance.

Don't worry too much about the specific choices you make. Your personal cloud will be malleable. Swap out bits as you like. If you choose poorly, just choose again (ideally based on metrics and user needs).

You aren't a failure if you don't get it right the first time.

It is OK to slowly migrate from whatever you currently use. No need to upset everything all at once.

It is OK to *not migrate at all* and just follow this book to expand your own personal learning and experimentation.

It is OK if you don't adhere perfectly to your or someone else's ideals. Stick to your values while you question and develop these values. Enjoy your journey.

3.1. Why you should self-host

Ask again—as you should—why the heck would anyone self-host software services? So many reasons!

- Flexibility
    - run only the services you and your users want
    - use multiple services backed by the same data storage
    - automate what you want, when you want
    - unlimited sharing
    - unlimited streaming
    - unlimited choices
- Fun!
    - learn and grow
    - self-hosting is a doable challenge
    - solve right-sized puzzles as you learn and improve
    - be part of the thriving self-hosting community
- Be future-proof
    - insulate your users from the unpredictable shifting of proprietary product prices, service offerings, and UI/UX
    - share your hard-earned data to your friends and family, forever
    - migrate to something else easily if and when you need to (for example, using a newer/better photo server once one becomes available)
    - it's really the *data* that must be safeguarded, the frontends to those data (file viewers, editors, etc) will change when *you* choose
- Democratize computing
    - self-hosted software (especially FOSS) enables data and

computational autonomy

- Conserve electricity
    - backend cloud power per device drops dramatically with a few users
    - save even more power the more users you add
    - see linked articles in Section 7.2.1, "Server"
- Save money
    - self-hosted hardware will typically beat cloud (renting someone else's)
    - savings increase as your users' data storage requirements enter the terabyte range
    - save more with every service you run
    - avoid unexpected public cloud costs
        - egress fees make it expensive to download your data and move it somewhere else
        - forgetting to shut down a VM (virtual machine) can get expensive quickly
        - you could spend excessive time and money navigating the public cloud's confusing menu of service offerings
    - avoid unexpected public clouds changes
        - changes in license fees
        - changes in usage fees
        - changes in support costs
        - changes in service offerings
    - near-zero incremental cost of adding users and services
- Speed / Save time
    - a nearby server can have much better response times, assuming reasonable hardware and well-behaved services

- nearby data ("data locality") means you don't need round-trips to someone else's data center to run experiments
- shared storage allows you to front your data with multiple services, choosing read-write/read-only access sensibly

- Avoid vendor lock-in
  - you'll be able to use software features public cloud providers don't offer or don't yet exist because you fully own and control your raw data
  - when you buy something with DRM, you don't really own it
  - is there an integration you count on? Sometimes a service stops working with another service. This happens less often with FOSS because anyone can simply fork (copy, modify, and share) a project.

- Privacy
  - avoid the chilling effect of mass surveillance
  - with a personal cloud you can safely and confidently keep GPS latitude and longitude in your photo metadata
  - once you keep your location metadata, you can do creative things with it
  - if you don't *need* to share your location and behavior with Google every second, why do you?
  - remove yourself from the equation of user analysis data—when you stream video from someone else's service, they know and analyze every time you (or your kids) (re-)watch a video you "own", every time you rewind, fast-forward, pause... but do they need to? why?

- Unlock new possibilities
  - apply arbitrary workflows to uploaded files
  - deploy trustworthy, offline generative AI (artificial intelligence) models

- enjoy features that don't exist in public services

3.2. Why you should not self-host

Self-hosting is more complex and time-consuming than paying for the same functionality, especially at first. It takes discipline and patience, like learning a new instrument (but *this* instrument eventually plays itself!).

If something breaks, you're fixing it. Sometimes you get a useful error, sometimes you can search the web for a quick fix. Sometimes you don't and can't.

 If you don't enjoy troubleshooting and debugging, self-hosting might not be for you.

If you don't take care with backups and security, you'll risk time, energy, and trust with people you care about.

On-premise self-hosting entails additional meatspace-specific considerations. You need to ensure sufficient power, connectivity, HVAC (heating, ventilation, and air conditioning), and security. Just don't keep your server outside.

4. Practical examples

I use lots of software during my daily routine. I'll need to look something up, get a ride, buy food, and so on. Much of this software is, sadly, quite annoying! It always seems to want more of my time, attention, and money, when I only want the practical outcome it purports to help me achieve. As a result I trust it less and constantly think of how I might replace it with something I like and trust more.

Here are a couple examples where I've improved on a public service with something self-hosted, followed by some surprises I encountered along the way.

4.1. Criminal chickens

My family has a homemade chicken safety system and the videos are important to me. I used to just plop them on YouTube because hey, it's free and it "just works", right?

Except when it doesn't. YouTube sometimes felt my chickens were being spammy, deceptive, and/or scammy.

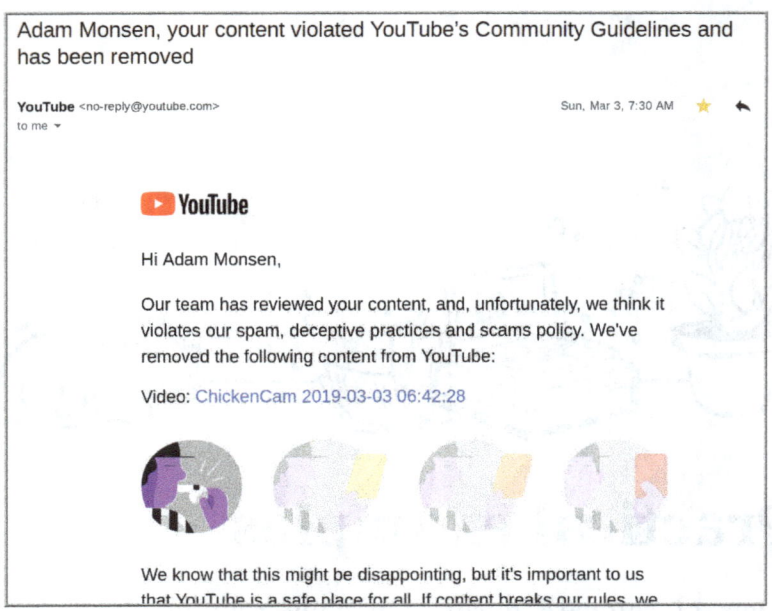

Figure 3. Screenshot of an email from YouTube content team having removed my chicken coop camera video.

For the record, our chickens are *squeaky clean.*

Figure 4. One absolutely upstanding, hard-working, law-abiding chicken.

Once I stood up my personal cloud I felt freedom and ease when posting and hosting these videos. I no longer needed to complete any

YouTube paperwork to be able to keep an eye on my chickens. I can safely ignore their audit and its erroneous policy violation claim.

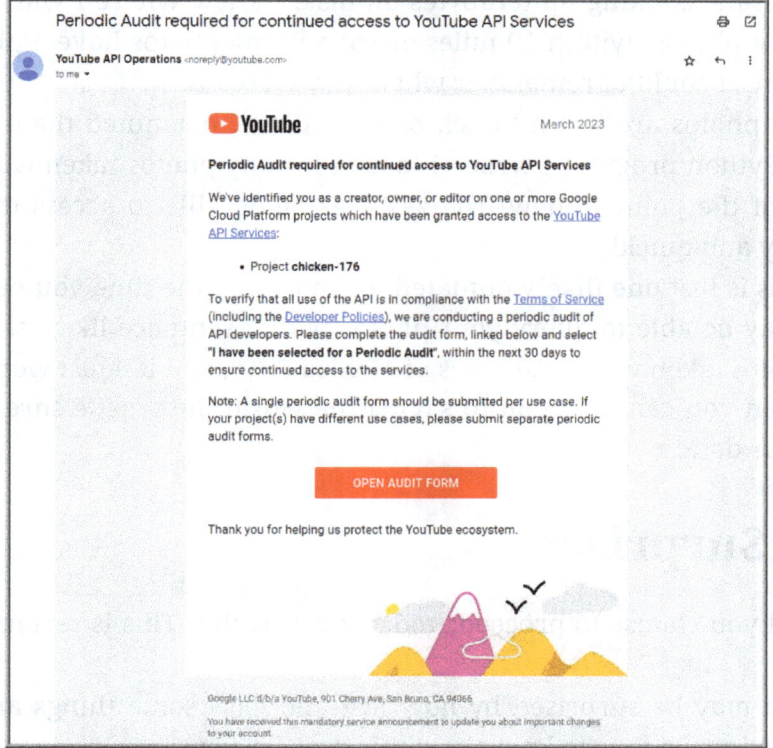

Figure 5. Screenshot of a YouTube legal audit for my old API client.

I also no longer need to work with YouTube's API (application programming interface), including registering an API client and completing periodic audits. After standing up Nextcloud I deleted my YouTube API client to upload videos, cleaning up my code and simplifying its maintenance. Turns out the Nextcloud Talk API is easier for posting my chicken coop photos and videos anyway.

With my own cloud I'm also able to tune quotas and rate limits as desired. Full speed ahead!

4.2. Photo search by location

Here's one more pro-personal-cloud example. This one worked because

I am comfortable storing location metadata in my self-hosted photos.

A while back I was trying to find some particular photos from a pile of thousands, taking up terabytes on disk. I knew where I was when I took the photos (within 10 miles or so) and my photos have embedded locations. I couldn't remember when they were taken.

My photos are just a bunch of JPEG files. I examined them with a small Python program I wrote. I looked for any photos taken within 10 miles of the point I knew. The key was being able to access the data directly and quickly.

This is just one (likely outdated) example. By the time you read this you may be able to query your photos with a sentence like: "show me all photos taken within 10 miles of Mexico City", and it'll just work.

Then you can move on to saving the world. Just make sure you've got your data!

4.3. Surprises

Should you choose to proceed: godspeed, traveler. This is seriously fun stuff.

You may be surprised by how fast and easy some things are with self-hosting. I'd love to know how this goes for you.

You may also be surprised by how time-consuming and difficult some things are. Maybe you'll get held up with hardware (and its power, wires, cooling, failures). Maybe networking. Maybe "change management" (trying to convince your users to use Nextcloud instead of Dropbox).

Here are some things that surprised me, both positively and negatively.

4.3.1. Good surprises

Hardware wasn't that hard

With help from a friend (thanks Rob!), I bought a reliable and cheap refurbished server. I thought I'd be tinkering with wires, cards, and

CMOS batteries. Not so! I opened the chassis to see the guts. I confirmed the contents were normal server guts, or close enough. The CPUs and memory sticks were all there as advertised.

I plugged it in; it worked.

Figure 6. View inside the server showing two empty PCI-E card slots.

Containers == happy

I was pleasantly surprised by containers (explained in Section 6.5, "Contained services") following my varied earlier experiences with VMs. VMs are simple at first because they behave much like physical hardware. Installing Linux into a VM is as easy as installing it onto bare metal (sometimes even easier). Then you can set up one or more services in the VM. The real rub here is with maintenance; maintaining a VM can be as complex as maintaining a bare metal server.

Containers take a different approach and simulate much less of a bare metal server. They are fast and small compared with VMs, allowing higher non-conflicting service density. That is, you can stand up more services per server and they don't interfere with one another (e.g. by requiring different versions of PHP (PHP: Hypertext Processor)). One container typically contains only one service.

Isolation of containers is limited compared to VMs. The kernel (the part of the OS that talks directly with the underlying hardware) is shared, for example. Limited isolation keeps the resource and maintenance costs of container-based isolation low compared with VMs.

Containers are excellent for a consistent and resilient personal cloud. They are easy to declare (in code), build, deploy, test, and repeat. They can also be used along with VMs: you might use a VM as your server instead of bare metal.

I chose Docker to manage containers because it is popular and I have experience with it. Your server is also considered a *host* since it it is a *host* to Docker containers.

One downside of Docker is how often root access is assumed in example code and popular public images. Running as `root` makes containers simpler but less secure.

Go paperless with OCR

Another smile-worthy advancement is free OCR (optical character recognition). I keep trying to "go paperless" by scanning in all my paper files. After scanning papers I am shouldered with, unsurprisingly, a bunch of PDFs of images. These can be easily OCR'd and managed with tools like Paperless-ngx [https://docs.paperless-ngx.com/] and Nextcloud Full text search [https://apps.nextcloud.com/apps/fulltextsearch].

Jellyfin works well

Jellyfin is a personal streaming media server. I was stoked to see how Jellyfin showed up as an excellent and complete FOSS alternative to Plex.

4.3.2. Bad surprises

Traefik learning curve

The Traefik reverse proxy was surprisingly challenging to set up because my networking fundamentals were rusty. I've got it working reliably and I still need to keep improving my fundamental knowledge in networking.

See Section 6.6, "Reverse Proxy" for more about Traefik.

Nextcloud bugs

I was frustrated with some bugs in Nextcloud. These felt like the most urgent since I rely heavily on it.

Community support is hit or miss. Nextcloud seems more popular outside the USA.

Not all Nextcloud apps are ready for prime time. See Section 10.8.7, "Customization".

Jitsi and ports

Jitsi is a self-hostable FOSS video call platform. I gave up trying to get Jitsi running in Docker. I recall lots of open ports or port ranges being a problem. This service might be easier to self-host in a virtual machine.

There's also a workaround assigning port ranges to specific IP addresses, but this is beyond the scope of this book. I will eventually give it another shot because logging in is now required when using the free 8x8-hosted Jitsi service [https://jitsi.org/blog/authentication-on-meet-jit-si/].

4.3.3. Absorb them all

When it comes to surprises, try to absorb the bad ones when they affect your users. Ideally *before* they affect your users, via research, planning, and testing you're likely already doing.

Dogfood what you self-host. Try your best to ensure everything is attractive and useful, then wait. Be patient. Never try to force people to use whatever you self-host.

I hope this book inspires you with many positive surprises and helps you and your users avoid many negative ones.

5. Plan

We'll now briefly cover the salient points of a self-hosting plan. I love this part! I get excited about what's to come, and I know a solid plan makes a vision real.

Make *your* plan. Maintain and improve your plan along with your server. Share the plan with other admins.

Yes, other admins. You need someone to cover for you when you are not available, or a crystal clear expectation that when you die, the server dies too.

5.1. Budget

Consider the time and cost of self-hosting. To yourself *and your users*. How much do you have and want to spend? Write down a number and stick to it.

5.2. Resources

Sketch out your thoughts on resources you'll need. Some ideas:

Compute and memory
CPU and RAM are the fundamental resources necessary for

computation. See Section 7.1.2, "Map services to resources" for ideas on how to estimate requirements based on the services you'll host. GPU workloads are not covered in this book, although Chapter 10, *What's next?*, and Chapter 13, *Exercises* touch on a few things you might try on your own.

Data storage

Estimate how much storage space you'll need. There's a significant jump in complexity and cost with each jump in unit (for example, GB (gigabyte) to TB (terabyte)). This book is appropriate for data storage up to about 10 TB. See Section 7.2.4, "Hard drives" for how to spend less on storage by self-hosting.

Electricity

Check your home power bill for the cost per kWh and run some estimates. See Section 7.2.1, "Server" for an example of the power used by a capable server.

Support

Who will help you when you get stuck? Section 11.1, "Support" has some ideas.

Physical location

Where will the server live? Will you have to install new wiring for power or network? Section 7.2.5, "Networking" covers my home setup.

5.3. Schedule

Rough out key dates so you and your users can plan ahead. For example:

Apr 28

Brainstorm, plan.

Apr 30

Order hardware.

May 3

Pull ethernet from router into garage.

May 5

Set up server: Install hard drives, power on, install OS, start services.

Jun 9

Review result against original goals.

Invite others to participate, starting at the beginning when you brainstorm and plan. This is a great time to include other people who may help care for the server.

5.4. Transition

Your users already have their data somewhere else. Consider how you'll help them migrate their data onto the server.

The key to this is excellent communication. Include this in your plan and seek buy-in since migration cost is a reality for every transition.

 To learn more about gracefully transitioning users between systems, study *change management*.

5.5. Sysadmin mindset

The server exists for the users. It is important to establish the right mindset to be able to provide an excellent user experience.

Make sure your self-hosted services work well for your users. Solicit their input often and take it seriously. Carefully tease out their *wants* vs. their *needs*.

Translate the word "users" as necessary. Perhaps: "those most dear to you, those you care about most above all others, those who give you meaning and purpose." Yeah, that's way over the top. You get the point: we must be thoughtful about what users experience or it will be frustrating for everyone.

Ideally you already know your users in real life. Stay connected with them in real life to better support them online.

6. System design

Let's dive into the design of a *Steadfast* system.

6.1. Service stack

A *Steadfast* system presents nicely as a simplified stack of colored boxes. The vertical ordering of the stack is based on where and how frequently a sysadmin will likely act and investigate at that layer when supporting or troubleshooting (most frequently at top), and amount abstracted from bare metal (least at bottom).

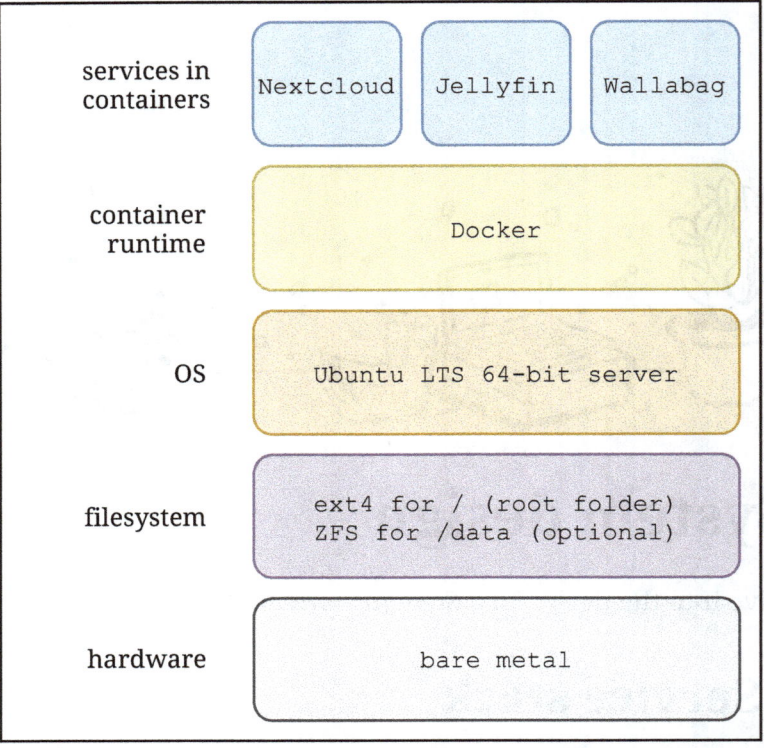

Figure 7. Layers of a Steadfast system. From the bottom, hardware: bare metal, filesystem: ext4 for / and optionally ZFS for /data, OS: Ubuntu LTS 64-bit server, container runtime: Docker, containers: Nextcloud file sharing app, Jellyfin media server, Wallabag article reader.

I am most often working around the top layers e.g. adding or updating a container. Less often I am updating OS (operating system) packages. Less often still I might examine versions of a configuration file stored on disk from its ZFS automatic snapshots. Finally, when my server dies, I'll be on that bottom layer fixing or replacing hardware. Here's where to look for details on each layer:

- services in containers:
    - Section 9.1, "Nextcloud: file sync and share"
    - Section 9.2, "Jellyfin: stream audio and video"
    - Section 9.3, "Wallabag: save and read articles"

- container runtime:
    - Section 4.3.1.2, "Containers == happy"
    - Section 6.5, "Contained services"
- OS: Section 6.4, "Operating system"
- filesystem: Section 6.3, "Filesystem"
- hardware: Section 7.2.1, "Server"

There are also two services in containers covered later and *not* pictured in the diagram:

- Section 9.4, "Watchtower: service updater"
- Section 9.5, "Scratch: visual programming"

6.2. Digital security

Let's cover the basic tools for understanding and securing your server.

6.2.1. Categorize your data

First, consider your data. It helps to break it down into two common categories:

Sensitive data

Examples: passwords, credit card numbers, government ID numbers. Recommendations:

1. Store offline only if possible.
2. If ever saved on a computer, store encrypted.
3. Easy fix: store in a password manager.

Everything else

Examples: notes, photos, documents, personal information. Recommendations:

1. Store on encrypted media, including backups.
2. Access only with up-to-date software you trust.
3. Disallow WAN (wide area network) access to these data.

6.2.2. WAN access

Once you've categorized your data, think about how people will get to it. At home you can generally just connect directly to your server. When you're away or you're trying to share with someone else, you're talking WAN access.

WAN access is—informally—remote access to services and data running in your LAN. One means of allowing WAN access to a service is by port forwarding HTTPS traffic through your router/firewall. Port forwarding without taking additional security measures is both risky and convenient.

> Consider alternatives to port forwarding, such as using a VPN.

6.2.3. Threat model

Let's back up a step and talk about threat modeling. Your *threat model* is how you'll consider threats to your data and how you'll mitigate these threats. With your threat model in mind, you'll be able to gain confidence in, for example, the decision of whether or not you should permit WAN access.

> If you already know you are a valuable target (public figure, high net worth, wartime journalist, responsible for a server with information about many people), buckle up for a longer journey. This guide is not sufficient for your threat model.

Let's build a simple example threat model for the "everything else" data class. Consider:

Assets

Data you are trying to protect.

Actors/Threats/Vectors

People and bots acting badly, and their means of attack. Includes mistakes and bugs.

Mitigations

Steps taken to reduce chances attacks succeed.

Put it all together and you get my 100% marketing-friendly threat model acronym **A.A/T/V.M.** (all punctuation is vocalized). Really just rolls off the tongue!

6.2.4. Example: WAN access

Test WAN access with this threat model.

Assets

Files with personal information stored in out-of-date service (e.g. an old, vulnerable version of Nextcloud).

Actors/Threats/Vectors

Bot scrapes websites and finds URL to service on a public mailing list archive. Bot automatically attempts exploit against known vulnerability in service. Exploit succeeds, bot owner gains access to compute resources and personal information.

Mitigations

Keep service up to date. Secure WAN boundary: monitor traffic logs, employ an IPS (intrusion prevention system), only cross into LAN using a VPN (virtual private network). Close WAN boundary: disallow all inbound WAN access.

Should you choose to expose a service, these mitigations will help secure it. "Avoid public mailing lists" is not listed in mitigations as it only obscures the URL to the out-of-date service, and one shouldn't rely on "security through obscurity".

Mitigating at multiple layers (OS firewall, service, WAN boundary) demonstrates "defense in depth", a common and worthwhile security practice.

6.2.5. VPN

A VPN can secure your WAN boundary by only allowing authenticated users and adding a layer of encryption. You can safely teleport back into your LAN while you are remote.

If all your users are able to use a VPN, you can keep ports closed for HTTP/S traffic and instead only allow VPN traffic. Assuming your VPN server is well-configured and up to date, this is an excellent way to reduce your attack surface.

VPN technology enjoyed a major upgrade with Wireguard [https://www.wireguard.com]. From a user perspective there's no heavyweight login process, as with older VPNs. Wireguard is fast, easy, and secure.

6.2.6. Full-disk encryption

Encrypting prevents data recovery by an attacker. You'll have to enter a password on boot, though. This is inconvenient if you have intermittent power and/or no remote management capability. There's also the reasonable argument that full-disk encryption offers little for an always-on server: during normal operation you've already supplied the decryption key.

If you decide you want full-disk encryption, choose it during Section 7.3, "OS install". Review the material earlier in this chapter if you want help with your decision.

6.2.7. More tips

Self-hoster security tips

- Maintain useful encrypted backups. Perform test restores to

prove they are useful. See Section 7.4.4, "Backups".
- Avoid running commands as the `root` user.
- Use multi-factor authentication.
- Use firewalls.
- Use strong passwords.
- Be very careful when port forwarding or don't do it at all.
- Be vigilant about all the usual stuff too: phishing, malware, SMS spoofing, and social attacks.
    - Take caution with email links and attachments.
    - Don't install untrusted software. Always use HTTPS.
    - Use a special passphrase with your mobile carrier as an extra layer of authentication.
    - Question urgency and suspicious requests.
- Send unrecognized calls to voicemail.
- Pay attention to data breaches and protect your identity.
    - Freeze your credit after a breach.
- Learn about compartmentalization and the principle of least privilege.

Further reading:

- Personal Cybersecurity: How to Avoid and Recover from Cybercrime [https://oreilly.com/library/view/personal-cybersecurity-how/9781484224304/] by Marvin Waschke
- Personal Privacy Threat Modeling (With LOTS Of Examples) [https://modernprivatelife.com/how-to-choose-privacy-threat-model/] by Eliza
- How I learned to stop worrying (mostly) and love my threat model [https://arstechnica.com/information-technology/2017/07/how-i-learned-to-stop-worrying-mostly-and-love-my-threat-model/] by Sean Gallagher

6.3. Filesystem

I recommend (and will demonstrate) starting with one ext4 filesystem and, optionally, one ZFS filesystem. ext4 is the stable, simple, and default filesystem for Ubuntu. ZFS (originally: Zettabyte File System) provides encryption, lightweight snapshots and RAID (redundant array of inexpensive disks).

You may optionally use ZFS for storage (`/data`) on your server following Section 7.3.1, "ZFS setup". For the root (`/`) partition, I recommend using ext4 instead of ZFS to:

- stick as closely as possible to the default Ubuntu install
- avoid Docker filesystem clutter
  - when `/var/lib/docker` is on ZFS, many Docker-related filesystems are created, cluttering up `zfs list` a bit
- avoid taking ZFS snapshots of the OS, since
  - we don't need to
  - the OS will live outside ZFS folders
  - we won't modify the OS—changes will be managed upstream (e.g. during package updates or via mario)

Docker volumes (persistent container data) will be on ZFS. The container's filesystem—everything besides mounted volumes with persistent data—is ephemeral and stored on ext4 in `/var/lib/docker`. To learn more about ZFS, see:

- Bitrot and atomic COWs: Inside "next-gen" filesystems [https://arstechnica.com/information-technology/2014/01/bitrot-and-atomic-cows-inside-next-gen-filesystems/] by Jim Salter
- ZFS 101—Understanding ZFS storage and performance [https://arstechnica.com/information-technology/2020/05/zfs-101-understanding-zfs-storage-and-performance/] by Jim Salter
- ZFS (Debian wiki page) [https://wiki.debian.org/ZFS] by various authors

Other ZFS concepts worth learning about: fragmentation, ARC (adaptive replacement cache), resilvering, scrubbing, `ashift`, and `recordsize`.

6.4. Operating system

Linux is a popular and reasonable choice for self-hosting. I recommend a 64-bit Ubuntu Linux server with at least 2GB memory and 30GB storage. Ubuntu LTS (long-term support) releases are the most stable and I recommend them. *Steadfast* specifically mentions 24.04, the LTS release from April 2024. 24.04 is stable today, and will receive updates until April 2034 [https://ubuntu.com/about/release-cycle], promising many more years of stability until *Steadfast* must be revised. Installing the OS is generally quick and painless, see Section 7.3, "OS install".

6.4.1. Customizations

It's good practice to minimize and carefully track customizations to the operating system from a default install. This eases maintenance, including eventual re-installs. Not mucking about on the server takes discipline, especially for old-school hands-on sysadmins like me.

Try to avoid SSH'ing into the server and making one-off changes. You'll learn how to instead modify mario's configuration files and re-provision the server in Chapter 8, *mario*.

You can and should still SSH into the server, but when you do, try to only run read-only or exceptional read-write commands. I often do something manually, undo it, then do the same thing with mario to confirm results are as expected.

> Example read-only server-side operations:
> - show per-container resource usage: `sudo docker stats`
> - follow container log messages: `sudo docker compose logs -f` (run this in a folder containing a `compose.yml` file)
> - check server health: `date; tail /proc/pressure/*`

> Example read-write server-side operations:
>
> - upgrade OS packages: `sudo apt full-upgrade`
> - change permissions for a folder: `chmod 0700 ~/bin/`

Start a "monthly maintenance" checklist like the one found in Section 7.4, "Server maintenance". Include these read-write operations in your checklist. Whenever possible, use mario to perform read-write operations.

Always use `sudo` to run privileged commands instead of logging in as `root`. This ensures every command is captured in `/var/log/auth.log` along with when it was executed, and by whom.

Upgrades may be automated. This is appropriate once you have sufficient scale (along with trust and control of the source of the upgrades). I usually do OS upgrades manually because I manage few systems so the burden is minimal and infrequent, and upgrading a package may require testing or manual intervention (e.g. rebooting). These reasons are similar to the reasons I install the OS itself by hand.

My OS is more a pet than cattle (see "cattle vs. pets" in Glossary). Perhaps it is a pet phoenix. When it dies, it will be relatively easy to revive from the ashes. It is backed up, there are few manual steps to perform, and all the manual steps are carefully documented.

6.5. Contained services

mario uses Docker to run services in containers. Docker is but one of many valid choices for how to isolate and run services. VMs are also often used for this purpose. See Section 4.3.1.2, "Containers == happy" for a comparison of the two. If you're interested in VMs (instead of or in addition to containers), check out Proxmox [https://proxmox.com].

Kubernetes also works well for running services. Try Kubernetes (especially one of the interesting micro-versions) if you are more familiar or interested in that. I found it to be overkill. If I needed high availability via clustering I'd be more likely to use Kubernetes. If one computer in a Kubernetes cluster breaks, services can automatically migrate to working hardware in the cluster. Regardless of your tech choices, set a clear expectation to your users as to how long your server might be down when something breaks.

Docker balances features and usability well, making it easy to run one service in isolation. Docker Compose adds the ability to define and run the groups of processes necessary to support a whole service (e.g. a web server and its database). Kubernetes can do this too, along with everything you *don't* need to learn unless you are building out an entire virtual data center. Docker Compose is a good fit for a single-server setup.

It is also good to avoid intermingling services and their dependencies along with everything else on the server's primary storage. Having everything on one filesystem is easy at first, for one service. It gets more complicated the more services you add [https://en.wikipedia.org/wiki/Dependency_hell].

Many of the desperate self-hoster support requests I see in FOSS communities are about incompatibilities between this or that version of PHP or relational database between two different services. Docker mitigates this by bundling dependencies. Each Docker image is basically a complete filesystem (sans kernel), so a service's image would always include the correct PHP version. Another image would be used to create the database, if/as necessary.

It's worth lingering on bundled dependencies for a minute. If dependencies are clothes, a Docker container is a strong and cheap suitcase with all the clothes you need for a week's travel. You check your suitcase and board the train, then rest easy knowing your suitcase is tucked neatly, separately, next to all the others. Docker containers are suitcases while the old way is everyones' unfolded clothes in a giant pile in the caboose.

Containers are created from images. An image is the blueprint to magic a fresh new suitcase (container) into existence, all packed and ready with the right clothes for your trip. An image is built once, stamped with an identifier, and shared, where it can act as the basis for countless consistently-behaving containers.

Images are defined by a file named `Dockerfile`. The `Dockerfile` should be tracked in source control. Since mario uses Docker Compose, another important file is `compose.yml`. Each service will have its own `compose.yml` file. These should be kept in source control too. For sysadmins these conventions provide reproducible images and containers. For users: predictable, reliable services.

Practice treating containers as temporary things. You'll gain confidence in your system by creating and destroying them frequently, and you'll enjoy the speed and ease of doing so. Think:

- ephemeral
    - containers are temporary
    - temporary containers provide robust, reproducible services
- cattle, not pets
    - hand-managed VMs are burdensome pets
    - apologies to the cattle—in this analogy they are expendable
- stateless
    - persistent data can and must be defined explicitly
- phoenix server
    - a term by Kornelis Sietsma describing repeated server destruction and re-creation

6.6. Reverse Proxy

A reverse proxy sits in front of containers and directs traffic to the right service based on arbitrary rules.

Say you've purchased the domain example.com and want to host Nextcloud at cloud.example.com and Jellyfin at jellyfin.example.com. Your sever uses a reverse proxy and a single IP address to direct incoming traffic to each of these services based on the hostname.

mario uses Traefik for its reverse proxy.

6.6.1. Traefik architecture

Here's a bit about how Traefik works and how it works with Nextcloud and other self-hosted web services.

We want HTTPS requests to port 443 bound for cloud.example.com to reach the Nextcloud service. Study the included Traefik architecture diagram to better understand this process along with the mario sources.

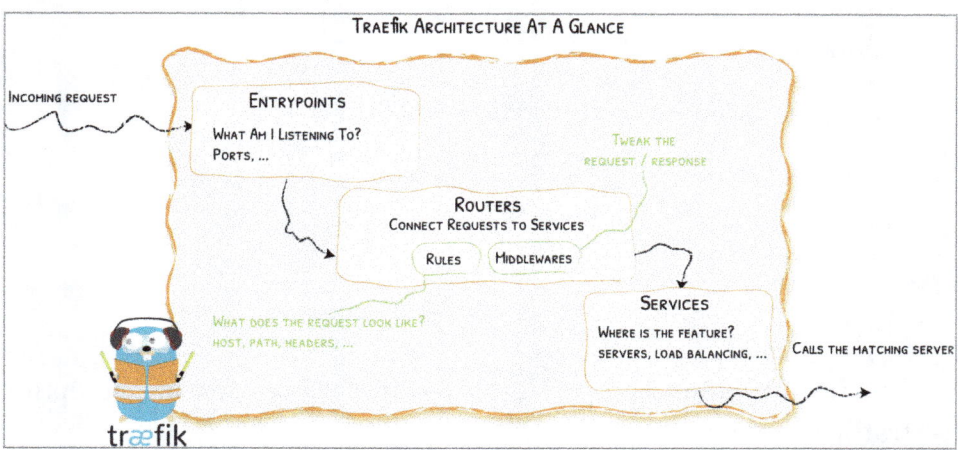

Figure 8. Traefik architecture diagram showing how a request reaches a service. From the MIT-licensed Traefik source code. Credit to Peka for the gopher logo, licensed CC-BY-3.0.

In the mario source code (or the snippets appearing later), look at the `compose.yml` files for Traefik and Nextcloud, which include:

- the `websecure` entrypoint, where we accept HTTPS traffic on port 443
- the `app` service definition for Nextcloud, which includes Traefik routing labels
- the `Host(⋯)` rule in the `nc-https` router

 The symbols `app`, `websecure`, and `nc-https` are arbitrary. I used short names to keep them from wrapping across lines. You may wish to use longer, more descriptive names.

The routing labels wire together the entrypoint and router with the service under which they are defined. That is: `websecure` to `nc-https` to `app`.

These two snippets of the mario source show how we set up Traefik for Nextcloud.

Listing 2. Traefik and Nextcloud configuration snippets (🏠 admin computer)

```yaml
# snippet from traefik/compose.yml
services:
  reverse-proxy:
    command:
      - --entrypoints.websecure.address=:443  ①

# snippet from nextcloud/compose.yml
services:
  app:
    labels:
      - "traefik.http.routers.nc-https.entrypoints=websecure"  ②
      - "traefik.http.routers.nc-https.rule=Host(`cloud.example.com`)"  ③
```

① Define entrypoint `websecure` on the `reverse-proxy` service, accepting traffic over port 443.

② Connect the `websecure` entrypoint with the `nc-https` router on the `app` service.

③ Use the hostname rule with the `nc-https` router.

Each self-hosted service will have its own router. Other web services will also use the `websecure` entrypoint.

HTTPS encryption is configured using other labels on the Traefik container. See Section 8.6, "Encryption certificates" for details.

7. Implementation

Now we're ready to stand up the first three layers in Section 6.1, "Service stack": Hardware, filesystem, and OS. I'll start by providing tools to evaluate services, then continue to OS installation and server maintenance.

7.1. Service plan

Services are long-running software programs on your server. Some have an interface, some run in the background on a schedule. "Web services" are the ones you can connect to using a web browser or other tool speaking HTTP.

7.1.1. Choose services

Start by reviewing your earlier needs and plans and use the material below to guide your decisions on which services you'll run. You may also skip ahead to Section 7.2, "Prepare hardware" to continue on the path of using the services mario installs by default, then return to this section when you're considering other services to add.

Good for self-hosting

You'll find some services are better choices to self-host than others. The good ones will likely share at least some of these traits.

> ## Traits of Good Self-Hosted Services
>
> - Easy to install and self-hosting instructions exist.
> - Works with your preferred deployment method, e.g. has a popular and well-maintained Docker image, has instructions for integrating with Docker Compose and Traefik.
> - Community uses tools such as moderated chats, forums, news, mailing lists, and meetups.
> - Recent source code activity: releases, contributions, news.
> - Uses a FOSS software license.
> - Transparent about owners and sponsors.
> - Public roadmap, issue tracking, continuous integration, working demo, build scripts, bug/security bounties.
> - If you experience a problem you're able to easily find more information about it (e.g. existing issue in tracker, workarounds) by searching the web.
> - Well-organized, elegant code.
> - Useful and up-to-date documentation.
> - Mentions and compares itself with other similar services.
> - Well-documented, useful, and complete API.
> - Flexible and extensible (easy to customize and extend with plugins and such).

See also: Checklist: Self-Hosting Solution Viability in Section 11.2, "Alternatives to mario".

These traits are based on standard industry practice as well as my personal values and preferences. Your own list may differ if, for example, you don't prefer FOSS licensing or do prefer a particular programming language.

Bad for self-hosting

Here are some indications a self-hosted service might be one to avoid.

> **Traits of Bad Self-Hosted Services**
>
> - Unpopular, inactive, or poorly maintained.
>   - Few maintainers / contributors.
>   - Maintainers are inattentive to contributors.
> - Includes telemetry (phones home, collects statistics or usage data), especially without your consent and/or enabled by default.
> - Has known security vulnerabilities.
> - Confusing or opaque governance, roadmap, licensing, source control, contribution intake, issue tracking.
> - Sprawling complexity.
> - Difficult to fork.
> - Only geared towards enterprise: self-hosting instructions are complex or missing entirely.
> - Frequent annoying upsells/nags.
> - Intentional vendor lock-in.
> - Depends on closed/proprietary standards/services.
> - Open core [https://en.wikipedia.org/wiki/Open-core_model].

I'm going to pick on Nextcloud here a bit. Nextcloud has far more good traits than bad, but these are still worth mentioning.

First, their apparently non-FOSS build script. Nick's explanation [https://help.nextcloud.com/t/build-bzip-and-package-from-git/58341/2] for this makes sense: it is more convenient for them to hardcode secrets directly in the build script and keep the whole thing secret. But hardcoded secrets are bad practice, it may be an AGPL license violation to hide a build script, and it makes forking harder. It's good practice to visualize succession, to be prepared for an eventual fork and change of ownership. Nextcloud is a fork of ownCloud, after all (see Section 10.8.10, "Nextcloud vs. ownCloud").

Second, sprawling complexity. "Nextcloud" is not one thing, it is a collection of *many* software projects and services under various degrees of control by a single company. This complexity makes forking costly and time-consuming. Even switching between extant forks (say, migrating back to ownCloud from Nextcloud) may be complex. They are clearly *not* trying to lock in customers, but the complexity itself may ultimately have that effect.

7.1.2. Map services to resources

Here's an early, rough resource planning table I used. You can use this pattern to estimate your own resource needs. I go into detail about a few of these services later in the book.

Table 2. Example tally of services to hardware resources

Service	Purpose	Isolation	Cores	RAM
jellyfin	stream music	Docker	2	2
kahoot-clone	quiz game	Docker	0	0
poller	polls	Docker	0	0
backuppc	backups	none	0	0
taskd	task tracking	Docker	0	0
sftp	file transfers	none	0	0
syncthing	file sync	none	1	1
nextcloud	file sharing	Docker	2	2
minetest	game server	Docker	4	8
irssi	chat client	none	0	0
jitsi	video calls	Docker	2	2
wallabag	article saver	Docker	1	1

"Cores" represents relative peak compute requirements. RAM: peak memory, in GB. These were rough estimates based on published documentation. The estimates turned out to be accurate enough. I could see right quick I'd need something more powerful than the latest available Raspberry Pi. See Section 7.2.1, "Server" for more lessons learned about resource requirements.

7.2. Prepare hardware

It's called *hard*ware because these problems are *hard*. That's fun to say and, in my experience, false. While there is a learning curve for understanding basic computer hardware components and hardware can certainly fail, there are plenty of wonderfully positive aspects of hardware. For example:

- Hardware is tangible and behaves consistently.

- Just plug it in, turn it on, and it'll probably work.
- When it does work, it is quite satisfying.

7.2.1. Server

You'll need a server.

You can always pay for "compute" in someone else's cloud, but it'll end up costing more in the long run.

If you're in a hurry, you can start with pretty much any old desktop or laptop, or your own VM running on either. Use something more powerful and expandable than a Raspberry Pi, though. What if your users love it? How will you increase storage? What about bursty workloads? If you start with something too small you won't have enough speed nor expandability.

I've worked with quite a few different servers and I did my homework for this self-hosting adventure, so I had a decent idea of what I wanted. I chose something powerful, cheap, and fast with plenty of storage and room to grow. I sought professional commodity hardware for its replace-ability. It can handle a reasonable amount of bursty compute needs, including building Docker images, flurries of user activity, and some generative AI (even without a GPU).

I found a used refurbished 1U rackmount server on eBay for about $1,000. This is sometimes called "off-lease enterprise hardware". A 1U server is one rack unit [https://en.wikipedia.org/wiki/Rack_unit] tall, like a long pizza box. Tech companies dump these by the truckload so you can usually find a good deal. Mine has two 24-core CPUs and 128 GB RAM.

Figure 9. DIY rackmount server attached to garage ceiling. It's fun to look at and is out of the way, but I need a ladder for maintenance and it weighs about 50lbs.

The fans are *way* louder than a desktop, especially when it is under load. It is supposed to have decent ventilation, temperature and humidity regulation yet has so far been extremely hardy even below freezing and above 100°F for extended periods of time. It has several enterprise features to ease maintenance such as redundant power supplies, hot-swap drive bays, lots of sensors, and remote management via a web browser or IPMI.

Power consumption averages 130W, or about 1,140kWh per year; roughly $138.15 in Seattle. That's about as much as a bright incandescent light bulb, and it's a bit wasteful for one user. Five users though? ~228kWh/year each. That's less than the cloud server hardware required for a mobile device making use of Google's or Apple's clouds. Further reading on this topic:

- The Surprisingly Large Energy Footprint of the Digital Economy [https://science.time.com/2013/08/14/power-drain-the-digital-cloud-is-using-more-energy-than-you-think/] by Bryan Walsh
- The spiralling energy consumption behind your smart phone [https://theguardian.com/sustainable-business/2014/sep/10/energy-

consumption-behind-smart-phone] by Betsy Reed

- The secret energy impact of your phone [https://increment.com/energy-environment/the-secret-energy-impact-of-your-phone/] by Owen Williams

A rackmount server like mine can handle far more than 5 users, assuming they aren't all trying to transcode video.

It also makes a great heated perch.

Figure 10. Bird perched on server.

7.2.2. Admin computer

It's helpful to have a separate computer from your server to make changes. I usually run mario using a laptop as my admin computer.

7.2.3. Test devices

Your users will have their own computers and mobile devices (their *clients*). Maintain a couple of different clients so you have comparable environments to better help your users.

TIP: Be a user of the services you self-host. This is *dogfooding*. Dogfooding keeps you honest and helps you empathize with others.

7.2.4. Hard drives

I use HDDs (hard disk drives) for data storage, mainly as a cost-saving measure vs. public cloud storage or SSDs (solid-state drives). The cost of public cloud block storage far exceeds the gigabyte-hour cost of my HDDs. I priced out one month of 5TB HDD block storage on AWS at $228.10. With ZFS I'm also taking a snapshot (bascially a full local backup) *every fifteen minutes*. One month's worth of hourly snapshots (the closest comparable I could find) is another $310.68 on AWS. That's $535.67 total, which is about what I spent on my drives. So I broke even in a month and the drives should last *years*.

For redundancy I recommend using two of the same drive, mirrored (RAID 1). This also increases read performance (for most reads) and halves usable storage space.

HDDs are plenty fast when measured from the standpoint of self-hosted service response time. The OS (operating system) and services do well at caching data served, assuming the server has sufficient RAM. Remote backups can take a while, and that's fine.

I use one SSD for the OS and everything besides my photos/documents/etc, since start-up time for the OS is important and realizes far less benefit from the OS filesystem cache (especially at boot time).

An interesting alternative to HDDs is object storage. Nextcloud can use object storage directly, for example. There are many aspects to consider when comparing the two options, such as:

- cost of storage and egress (download)
- control, autonomy, sovereignty
- direct access to data
- speed and means of access
- network availability
- backups, versioning, security

I went with HDDs for direct, local access to my data. I really wanted to know exactly where they were stored and for ultimate flexibility when

I change or try new services. Most of my services require direct access anyway.

7.2.5. Networking

If you are hosting at home, you need a reliable WAN (wide-area network) connection if you want to be able to connect from other places besides your LAN. Use wired ethernet cables to your server, not Wi-Fi. A wired LAN is more reliable and easier to troubleshoot.

Minimum requirements

Here are some typical minimums for hosting at home:

- 100mbps up / 100mbps down ISP connection
- Cat 5 ethernet cable (for your server)
- 802.11ac Wi-Fi (for clients)

I just made these up based on what works for me, then doubled that so you have some room to grow.

Home router configuration

Learn how to configure your router. Keep it up to date and maintain a strict firewall with only the necessary ports open / forwarded.

> Port forwarding allows inbound connections through your WAN boundary to your server. Read Section 6.2, "Digital security" before forwarding any ports.

Make a sketch to better understand your network. Here's a simple diagram I created using asciiflow.com to plan cabling and visualize the flow of traffic through my network devices:

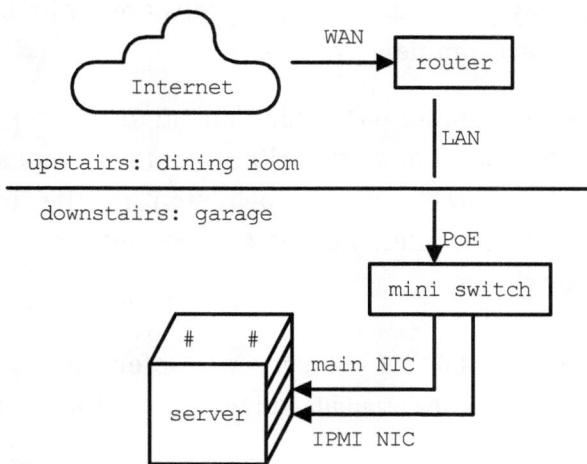

Figure 11. WAN into LAN traffic flow diagram.

Arrows represent ethernet cable. The router provides electricity to the mini switch using PoE (power over ethernet). The server has two NICs (network interface cards): one for the OS and everything within (including all services), and one for a network connection to the embedded OOB (out-of-band) remote management computer with IPMI (Intelligent Platform Management Interface). WAN traffic is allowed to flow to the main NIC and not to the IPMI NIC.

7.2.6. Electricity

Use a surge protector. Consider a UPS (uninterruptible power supply) if your power at home is unreliable.

7.2.7. Physical security

Keep your server safe, similar to other valuables in your home. At the very least, restrict physical access.

7.3. OS install

Here's a guide to setting up your server. The OS install takes about five minutes if everything proceeds smoothly. Steps are omitted for brevity when the default is acceptable.

 As you install the OS, think ahead to disaster recovery. Take notes and visualize yourself repeating the process precisely. At each step in the interactive Ubuntu installer, accept the default or write down your choice.

1. **Install Ubuntu** 24.04 LTS server. Refer to this tutorial [https://ubuntu.com/tutorials/install-ubuntu-server] for step-by-step instructions.

2. **Use a static IP address** when configuring networking. You may also be able to leave this as the default (DHCP/dynamic), and use your LAN router to assign an IP address that doesn't change.

3. Optional: use full-disk encryption. See Section 6.2.6, "Full-disk encryption".

4. **Note the username and password** when you set up a user account (called a "Profile" in the installer). You'll need these soon.

5. **Install OpenSSH server** when prompted to do so.

6. **Do not install Nextcloud or Docker**, let mario install these later.

Congratulations, you just installed Linux! Next steps:

1. Optional: after installing Ubuntu, add two HDDs and format them with ZFS. See Section 7.3.1, "ZFS setup".

2. Download mario onto your admin computer (a separate computer from your server). See Chapter 11, *More resources*.

3. Run mario on your admin computer to provision your server. See Chapter 8, *mario*.

7.3.1. ZFS setup

The OS takes care of itself pretty well. For more robust data storage, you can add a couple of HDDs and manage them with ZFS.

ZFS adds many features and some complexity. The learning curve is worth it. The guide below walks through creating a simple pool of two mirrored drives, visible at `/data`. This is a reasonable starting point, providing increased fault tolerance and better read performance than a single drive.

On the server, run these commands as `root` (hint: use `sudo su -` first). The code below assumes you've added two drives and they were assigned `/dev/sda` and `/dev/sdb`, so adjust device names as necessary. Use `lsblk` to figure out your device names.

Listing 3. ZFS setup (🐦 server)

```
# Create partition tables.
parted /dev/sdb mklabel gpt
parted /dev/sdc mklabel gpt

# Create ZFS main mirrored pool and set attributes (for all future datasets
# in this pool).
zpool create -O mountpoint=none main mirror /dev/sdb /dev/sdc
# For performance.
zfs set atime=off main
# To save space.
zfs set compression=on main
# For security.
zfs set exec=off main
zfs set setuid=off main
zfs set canmount=off main

# Create encrypted dataset in "main" pool. This is the "parent" dataset, we
# can easily add more later and they'll all be encrypted.
openssl rand -base64 32 > /root/secure-dataset-key
zfs create -o encryption=on -o keyformat=passphrase \
    -o keylocation=file:///root/secure-dataset-key main/secure
zfs set canmount=off main/secure

# Create usable (mount-able) dataset.
zfs create -o mountpoint=/data main/secure/data

# This might not be necessary if you _never_ want to execute anything in
# /data. I found I needed it for something within a container (ffmpeg, I
# think). You can start with exec=off and turn it on later if you want.
zfs set exec=on main/secure/data
```

Here are a few commands to see details about what you just created. These do not require root access.

Listing 4. show ZFS details (🪶 server)

```
# Examine pools.
zpool status
zpool list

# Examine datasets.
zfs list
```

On Ubuntu 24.04 LTS, more steps are required to automatically mount this new filesystem when the server boots. What follows is from the `zfs-mount-generator(8)` manual page, with a few corrections. These must be run as `root`.

Listing 5. ZFS mount on boot setup (🪶 server)

```
# enable tracking for the pool
mkdir /etc/zfs/zfs-list.cache
touch /etc/zfs/zfs-list.cache/main

# enable the tracking ZEDLET
systemctl enable zfs-zed.service
systemctl restart zfs-zed.service

# trigger cache refresh
zfs set relatime=off main/secure
zfs inherit relatime main/secure

# re-run systemd generators and reboot
systemctl daemon-reload
reboot
```

7.4. Server maintenance

I use short monthly and yearly maintenance checklists. I update my checklists about as often as I use them. Here are examples you might use as starting points.

> **Checklist: Monthly Maintenance**
>
> ☐ Upgrade OS packages.
>
> ☐ Check storage space remaining.
>
> ☐ Back up router configuration.

> **Checklist: Yearly Maintenance**
>
> ☐ Test restore from backup.
>
> ☐ Review and improve threat model.
>
> ☐ Open server chassis and vacuum dead spiders.

The following sections cover specific maintenance tips and tricks.

7.4.1. Hardware failure

Plan on hardware failure. If you can afford it, the easiest way to reliably run one server is to *buy two identical servers*. Use the second for parts or a ready as-is replacement machine (also called a "cold spare").

7.4.2. Software updates

Keep your server up to date. For the OS:

Listing 6. *upgrade packages (🦅 server)*

```
sudo apt update && sudo apt full-upgrade
```

This will update local package information and—if that succeeded—upgrade the OS. Root access is required, hence `sudo`. This is relatively safe and typically requires little to no interaction besides a confirmation to proceed. A reboot may be required afterwards (e.g. when the kernel is upgraded). The server will say if a reboot is required upon login.

Each service in Chapter 9, *Services* includes a "Maintenance notes" section with update instructions. Container images can be updated by hand with Docker Compose or automatically by Watchtower. See Section 9.4, "Watchtower: service updater" for details.

7.4.3. Monitoring

Monitor server health. Check free disk space with `df -h`. If things feel slow, check PSI (pressure stall information) with

Listing 7. check PSI (🗲 server)

```
tail /proc/pressure/*
```

`atop` will also show PSI values. If your PSI check shows high resource usage, try `docker stats` to see resource usage per container. That should help you narrow down the issue to specific services.

If you are using ZFS, you can use `zpool iostat` to see input/output statistics for your storage pool(s).

At the host level, you can use `htop -d 100` to see stats for all processes and threads. Follow all logged events for the host with `journalctl -f`.

7.4.4. Backups

Having useful backups is one critically important practice you'll rarely get credit for doing well, only blame if it is done poorly.

Check your backups regularly to make sure they work.

Make consistent backups of everything on your server, such that the services running are unaware they are even being backed up. For example: create a ZFS snapshot and back *that* up.

Backing up using ZFS snapshots *can* still cause problems. For example, ZFS doesn't guarantee consistent state of backed-up data for running programs. Say you restored a MariaDB database from backup. Unless you flushed and locked tables before taking that ZFS snapshot, MariaDB might have been in the middle of a write operation with in-memory data not yet flushed to disk. It would need to recover, and the data MariaDB was trying to write may be lost. This manner of data loss is rare, and the risk is acceptable for the typical homelab.

 Create backups following the 3-2-1 rule of thumb: make **3** backups. Store at least **2** local copies on different media. Have **1** remote backup.

I recommend a backup strategy combining ZFS snapshots with either restic [https://restic.net] or Borg [https://borgbackup.org] for sending them offsite. Here's a decent comparison of restic vs. Borg [https://reddit.com/r/BorgBackup/comments/v3bwfg/].

Here are some example commands demonstrating how to back up a ZFS filesystem. You can use these to get started writing your own backup script.

Listing 8. example backup script (🪶 server)

```
snapName=$(date -I)-backup

sudo zfs snapshot main/secure/data@$snapName ①

sudo restic backup /data/.zfs/snapshot/$snapName ②

sudo zfs destroy -R main/secure/data@$snapName
```

① Running this command to create a snapshot takes 0.040 seconds on my server. Once it is done, a new read-only folder will appear under `/data/.zfs/snapshot` containing the snapshot.

② This line assumes you have installed and configured restic. It can send your snapshot offsite, following the 3-2-1 rule of thumb.

8. mario

mario is a tool I built to help you set up and maintain a server. It is mainly a wrapper around the well-established Ansible [https://ansible.com] system provisioner. Everything I'll do with mario can also be done manually, directly on the server. The advantage of using mario instead is that each change (say, installing a package) will be made consistently and with an audit trail. The real payoff of this practice is realized when you collaborate with others, including your future self. It's not often easy to remember what you did a year ago and why.

Once your server is online following Section 7.3, "OS install", use mario to configure and start services.

Please download the source code (see Chapter 11, More resources). It'll be helpful to have this handy so you can follow along as you read.

mario can be found alongside this book, in the `mario/` folder. The `provision.sh` script is in `ansible/`.

8.1. mario philosophy

mario is a practical learning tool. It comes with sensible, tested defaults. It automates some of the tedious, confusing steps of setting up services on a server. mario is not a supported and production-ready software product. It'll get you started, that's all. Continue with it if you like or just use it to fast-forward your personal cloud setup. Something else does or will do its job better. Here are some suggestions to get the most out of mario.

The first time you run mario, follow the instructions as closely as possible. Many assumptions are made so it works "out of the box", and it is meant to be easily customizable.

mario configuration files are declarative: They contain the *state* you want your server to end up at, not all the individual commands you'd run manually to achieve the same state. mario's `provision.sh` runs Ansible, and Ansible runs the commands for you on the server (like running `chmod` on a file) in a predictable and repeatable manner. The desired end state, as declared in the configuration files, is reached and confirmed by Ansible.

After getting mario up and running successfully once, run it again! Provisioning with mario is reassuringly idempotent: The system will not change in any meaningful way after the desired state is reached. Once `provision.sh` completes successfully, it may be re-run to confirm the server is still in the desired state. Then, start tinkering. You can find some ideas in Chapter 13, *Exercises*.

If you are familiar with and prefer using VMs, you may want to first create a VM and run mario against that until you're ready to run mario pointed at your real server. Or perhaps your real server *is* a VM—that'll work fine too.

8.2. SSH setup

mario runs on your admin computer and expects to be able to connect directly to your server using SSH. Here's how to get this working.

First, map your server IP address to a convenient name. Using the IP address from Section 7.3, "OS install", add a line like this to your hosts file (e.g. `/etc/hosts`):

Listing 9. line to add to hosts file (🏠 admin computer)

```
192.168.1.100    mario_server
```

Confirm you're able to ping the server using the name `mario_server`. Here's what it looks like when it works:

Listing 10. test ping server (🏠 admin computer)

```
$ ping mario_server
PING mario_server (192.168.1.100) 56(84) bytes of data.
64 bytes from mario_server (192.168.1.100): icmp_seq=1 ttl=64 time=0.316 ms
64 bytes from mario_server (192.168.1.100): icmp_seq=2 ttl=64 time=0.535 ms
64 bytes from mario_server (192.168.1.100): icmp_seq=3 ttl=64 time=0.178 ms
^C
--- mario_server ping statistics ---
3 packets transmitted, 3 received, 0% packet loss, time 2041ms
rtt min/avg/max/mdev = 0.178/0.343/0.535/0.146 ms
```

Next, make your SSH client pass along the correct username when you run `ssh mario_server`. Here's an example client configuration template for OpenSSH. Replace `your-username` with the account username on your server.

Listing 11. customize OpenSSH client configuration (🏠 admin computer)

```
Host mario_server
  User your-username
```

You can add that to `~/.ssh/config`, adapting as necessary for the SSH client you use. Test it by running `ssh mario_server`. You may see something like this:

Listing 12. SSH host fingerprint prompt (🏠 admin computer)

```
The authenticity of host 'mario_server (192.168.1.100)' can't be established.
ECDSA key fingerprint is SHA256:o2kUkvSP3JG9PTt/Ju11FWKkCpTJCB4rY3jQvImtRNw.
Are you sure you want to continue connecting (yes/no/[fingerprint])?
```

If the IP address is correct, it is safe to assume the LAN-only server you just created is the same one you're trying to connect to now. Go ahead and continue with yes + Enter . If you want to be super careful, run one of these commands on the server and confirm the fingerprints match:

Listing 13. show SSH host public key (server)

```
# use this if you saw "ECDSA key fingerprint..." earlier
ssh-keygen -lf /etc/ssh/ssh_host_ecdsa_key.pub

# use this if you saw "ED25519 key fingerprint..." earlier
ssh-keygen -lf /etc/ssh/ssh_host_ed25519_key.pub

# use this if you saw "RSA key fingerprint..." earlier
ssh-keygen -lf /etc/ssh/ssh_host_rsa_key.pub
```

Next, set up public key authentication. If you need a key pair, run ssh-keygen or similar on your admin computer to create one. If you already have a key pair, use it. Copy the public key to the server with ssh-copy-id or similar. For example:

Listing 14. install SSH key on server (admin computer)

```
$ ssh-copy-id mario_server
/usr/bin/ssh-copy-id: INFO: attempting to log in with the new key(s), to filter
out any that are already installed
/usr/bin/ssh-copy-id: INFO: 2 key(s) remain to be installed -- if you are
prompted now it is to install the new keys
mario2024@mario_server's password:

Number of key(s) added: 2

Now try logging into the machine, with:   "ssh 'mario_server'"
and check to make sure that only the key(s) you wanted were added.
```

Test that everything so far is working by running ssh mario_server. You should see something like this:

Listing 15. successful SSH to server (admin computer)

```
$ ssh mario_server
Welcome to Ubuntu 24.04 LTS (GNU/Linux 6.8.0-31-generic x86_64)

... snip ...
```

```
Last login: Fri May  3 16:44:52 2024 from 192.168.13.225
user@server:~$
```

8.3. Provision server

Run `provision.sh` on your admin computer (*not* on your server):

Listing 16. mario first run (🏠 admin computer)

```
cd mario/ansible
./provision.sh
```

On this first invocation, mario will check for prerequisites and prompt you to enter values specific to your server into a configuration file.

Listing 17. mario first run output (🏠 admin computer)

```
You don't have a config file. I'll create one for you now.

Please edit 'config' and re-run this script.
```

Here's a guide for settings in your `config` that must be changed from their defaults. Be sure to study the comments in that file, too. I'll assume you have a domain name and a DNS provider with an API. See Section 8.4, "Server domain name" for details on how to obtain this.

`DNS_API_PROVIDER`

    Enter the name of your DNS provider here. mario configures Traefik to talk directly with your DNS server for issuing Let's Encrypt certs.

`NAMECHEAP_*`, `DUCKDNS_*`, `R53_DNS_*`, `DO_*`...

    Enter credentials for only one provider, the same provider you specified in `DNS_API_PROVIDER`.

`DNS_RESOLVER_EMAIL`

    Enter an email matching what you use with your DNS API provider. You may receive emails from Let's Encrypt at this address.

`MARIO_DOMAIN_NAME`

> This will be a name like `example.duckdns.org` or `example.com`. Individual services will be named based on this, e.g. `jellyfin.example.com`.

Finish editing `config` and run `provision.sh` again. This run will ask you for the password you set during Section 7.3, "OS install" and subsequent runs will not. You should see output similar to this:

Listing 18. mario second run output (🏠 admin computer)

```
BECOME password:

PLAY [all] *********************************************************************

TASK [base : Configure apt cache] **********************************************
ok: [mario_server]

TASK [base : Install packages] *************************************************
changed: [mario_server]

... snip ...

PLAY RECAP *********************************************************************
mario_server              : ok=21    changed=0    unreachable=0    failed=0
skipped=3    rescued=0    ignored=0
```

It takes around ten seconds for mine to complete. All tasks will be `ok` in the recap for a fully provisioned system. Some tasks will be `skipped` until Nextcloud is started for the first time—ignore those for now.

If `provision.sh` completed without errors, mario was able to get your server and services ready to use. Proceed directly to Section 8.5, "Start services".

8.4. Server domain name

Your server needs a name. It gets a hostname during Section 7.3, "OS install", but this one doesn't matter so much for a *Steadfast* server. I recommend getting a domain name and naming all your services using subdomains (e.g. `cloud.example.com`). You can either use a free domain name or buy a domain name from a registrar. mario needs the domain name to be able to use a DNS provider with an API for setting up HTTPS web traffic encryption.

You may also want to be able to refer to your server by name when you're away from your LAN if you allow WAN access and/or if you have a dynamic WAN IP address. Check with your DNS provider about adding appropriate records for this purpose (e.g. `A` and `CNAME` records).

8.4.1. Public DNS

Duck DNS provides a free domain name and DNS service. mario also works with paid services such as Namecheap, DigitalOcean, and Route 53. I recommend any of the paid options over Duck DNS. Support for other DNS providers (ahem, especially self-hosted ones!) may be added later.

 Public DNS records do not presume WAN access. Section 6.2, "Digital security" covers WAN access in detail.

Duck DNS

If you want a free domain name from a provider with an API, you can try your luck with Duck DNS.

1. Start at duckdns.org.
2. Log in and add a domain.

Your domain will be named something like `blah.duckdns.org`. Use this in place of `example.com` as appropriate, e.g. use `cloud.blah.duckdns.org` for `cloud.example.com`.

Amazon Route 53

If you choose Route 53, create a new hosted zone with the domain name you own. Make note of the Route 53 name servers. Back at your registrar, input these name servers.

On Amazon IAM, create a user with permission to update this hosted zone. Here's a policy with way too much access that nevertheless works:

Listing 19. naive Route 53 policy

```
{
  "Version": "2012-10-17",
  "Statement": [
    {
      "Effect": "Allow",
      "Action": "route53:*",
      "Resource": "*"
    }
  ]
}
```

8.4.2. Dynamic DNS

If you want WAN access and your IP address changes periodically, it's handy to have this updated in DNS automatically. Similar to Traefik setting up HTTPS certs, this uses a DNS provider API. There are several options here, all left as exercises for the reader. One idea is to find and stand up a dynamic DNS client for your Docker image. These are generally very simple services to set up. Another idea is to see if your router will do the dynamic DNS updates.

8.4.3. Internal DNS

It is handy to have an internal DNS server to be able to refer to your server by name. These internal names should match the public names and point to LAN-only private IP addresses. This way you can use the same names inside and outside your LAN and your Let's Encrypt certs will work. Your LAN router likely has a DNS server and may allow you to assign names to IP addresses.

If you don't have an internal DNS server, you can create more hostname to IP address mappings like the one we added in Section 8.2, "SSH setup". Here's that hosts file again:

Listing 20. hosts file with service names (admin computer)

```
# for provisioning from admin computer
192.168.1.100    mario_server

# for accessing services from admin computer
192.168.1.100    traefik.example.com
192.168.1.100    cloud.example.com
192.168.1.100    jellyfin.example.com
192.168.1.100    wallabag.example.com
192.168.1.100    scratch.example.com
```

Manually mapping IP addresses to hostnames with a hosts file is handy for initial setup and maintenance when your internal DNS server fails. Remember that only the computer with these specific mappings will be able to use the names. Test the mappings using `ping` on your admin computer.

> 💡 I've shown examples of two styles of service domain names. `cloud.example.com` indicates the function of the service, rather than the service's brand name. `nextcloud.example.com` would work just as well. The choice is yours.

8.5. Start services

mario has prepared your server to run a handful of services. Docker and Docker Compose are installed. Docker configuration files are stored in directories under `/root/ops`. Data for services are stored in directories under `/data`.

None of the services are running yet. We'll soon get to how to turn them on and start using them.

Let's first take a step to save a lot of typing. Services are started and stopped with Docker Compose, which is always run with `docker compose`. When you run `docker compose`, you must first be in a folder containing a `compose.yml` file. By convention, the name of that folder is the name of the service. A typical usage pattern is:

Listing 21. start a service in its folder (🌱 server)

```
sudo su -
cd /root/ops/traefik
docker compose up -d
```

Try to avoid this method. The fewer commands you run directly as root, the better. I recommend this instead:

Listing 22. start a service, explicit configuration file (🌱 server)

```
sudo docker compose --file /root/ops/traefik/compose.yml up -d
```

mario installs a program called `dc` on the server to save you some typing:

Listing 23. start a service with dc (🌱 server)

```
# equivalent to
# sudo docker compose --file /root/ops/traefik/compose.yml up -d
dc traefik up -d
```

 sudo is required to run some commands, including `docker compose`. The `dc` script will run `sudo` for you.

8.5.1. Start reverse proxy

Stand up the reverse proxy first. On your server, start Traefik with `dc traefik up -d`. If that worked, wait a minute or two and visit https://traefik.example.com in a web browser to see the Traefik dashboard. While you are waiting for the dashboard, tail the logs with `dc traefik logs -f`.

It may take that minute or two for Traefik to set up Let's Encrypt HTTPS encryption certs, so don't worry if you get invalid cert warnings at first. You should see something like this for a working Traefik service:

Listing 24. typical Traefik logs, edited for brevity (🐦 server)

```
+ sudo docker compose --file /root/ops/traefik/compose.yml logs -f
rp-1 | Traefik version 3.0.0 built on 2024-04-29T14:25:59Z version=3.0.0
rp-1 | Starting provider aggregator aggregator.ProviderAggregator
rp-1 | Starting provider *traefik.Provider
rp-1 | Starting provider *docker.Provider
rp-1 | Starting provider *acme.ChallengeTLSALPN
rp-1 | Starting provider *acme.Provider
rp-1 | Testing certificate renew... acmeCA=... providerName=myresolver.acme
^Ccanceled
```

If you waited a bit, re-loaded the page, and are still getting invalid cert warnings from your browser when you try to visit https://traefik.example.com, read the Traefik log messages carefully and also see Section 8.6, "Encryption certificates" for troubleshooting steps. Once you're able to view the dashboard, stop tailing the Traefik logs with `Ctrl` + `c`.

8.5.2. Start other services

Starting a mario service is always done with `dc SERVICE up -d`, just like we did with Traefik. To stand up everything at once, you could use this shell script:

Listing 25. start all services ad-hoc Bash script (🐦 server)

```
for service in $(sudo ls /root/ops); do
    dc $service up -d
done
```

This will also pull and build images and update containers as necessary. Services out of sync with their `compose.yml` file will be restarted. This is idempotent: running and up-to-date services are left unchanged.

8.6. Encryption certificates

Traefik will automatically install Let's Encrypt certs to encrypt HTTP traffic. The certs are issued using a DNS challenge [https://doc.traefik.io/traefik/https/acme/#dnschallenge]. This way to authenticate a cert request [https://letsencrypt.org/docs/challenge-types/] is especially handy for servers with zero public-facing inbound ports, allowing convenient HTTPS even within closed LANs. The DNS challenge is configured using labels in Traefik's `compose.yml` configuration file.

Traefik can accept HTTPS, decrypt it, and pass along unencrypted HTTP to web services. This is called SSL termination, and is configured by lines in Traefik's `compose.yml` mentioning `acme`.

Take a look at a `compose.yml` file for any service included with mario. Every service has a `tls` section defined on its router to enable HTTPS encryption and SSL termination.

If you see cert warnings while trying to reach your web services, first examine Traefik logs as indicated in Section 8.5.1, "Start reverse proxy". To increase the Traefik log verbosity, change `--log.level=INFO` to `--log.level=DEBUG` in Traefik's `compose.yml`, re-provision, and re-start Traefik. To troubleshoot further, confirm DNS queries are succeeding since this affects the DNS challenge.

Listing 26. example DNS tests

```
####
# Try these commands on both the admin computer and server.
# Replace dig (and its arguments) with your favorite DNS tool.
# Replace traefik.example.com with your Traefik service name.
####

# Look up Traefik on default DNS server.
# Should quickly return a LAN private IP address.
dig traefik.example.com

# Look up Traefik server name on Quad9 DNS.
# - @9.9.9.9 forces Quad9's DNS service.
# - +short uses terse output
# Should return nothing--we didn't set an IP address.
dig @9.9.9.9 +short traefik.example.com

# Fetch TXT record for Traefik.
```

```
# Contains a long unique string while Traefik is executing a
# DNS challenge and is otherwise not set.
dig traefik.example.com TXT
```

8.7. Tiny test service

If you got this far, try standing up a test service. This is useful to confirm networking is functional for Docker containers running on your host. We likely already have this assurance if Traefik is working (since it requires networking for the DNS challenge), but this may still be a useful tool for another time, or at least a positive step towards creating your own useful services.

This service demonstrates pinging a public server. On *your* server, create the folder `~/ping/`. Create a file `compose.yml` in that folder, containing:

Listing 27. tiny test service config (🌱 server)

```yaml
version: '3'

services:
  test:
    image: alpine
    command: ping example.com
```

In the folder `~/ping/`, run the command `sudo docker compose up`. Hit `Ctrl` + `c` after a few seconds. You should see something like this:

Listing 28. start tiny test service (server)

```
$ cd ~/ping/
$ sudo docker compose up
[+] Running 2/2
 ✔ Network ping_default    Created                              0.1s
 ✔ Container ping-test-1   Created                              0.1s

Attaching to ping-test-1
ping-test-1  | PING example.com (93.184.216.34): 56 data bytes
ping-test-1  | 64 bytes from 93.184.216.34: seq=0 ttl=55 time=3.477 ms
ping-test-1  | 64 bytes from 93.184.216.34: seq=1 ttl=55 time=3.236 ms
ping-test-1  | 64 bytes from 93.184.216.34: seq=2 ttl=55 time=3.363 ms
^CGracefully stopping... (press Ctrl+C again to force)
Aborting on container exit...
[+] Stopping 1/1
 ✔ Container ping-test-1   Stopped                             10.4s
canceled
```

> 💡 For extra credit, incorporate your tiny test service into mario.

This is the basis for adding more interesting services, too. It's only a few more lines of code and configuration to create a small API or web service and a few more to publish it with your reverse proxy.

9. Services

Now you can try out the services provisioned by mario. This chapter covers what they provide and how to manage them.

Table 3. Purposes of default mario services

Purpose	See
sync and share files, groupware	Section 9.1, "Nextcloud: file sync and share"
stream music and home movies	Section 9.2, "Jellyfin: stream audio and video"
read articles offline, without distractions	Section 9.3, "Wallabag: save and read articles"
keep other services up to date	Section 9.4, "Watchtower: service updater"
learn to code with visual tools	Section 9.5, "Scratch: visual programming"

These particular services are a small fraction of those available to self-host. They reflect my users' preferences (including and over-indexed to my own) in reading, sharing, media, and so on. Getting them running will provide some useful functionality for your users and a good starting point for self-hosting whatever you want.

For each service you'll find my personal commentary and issues I encountered. If I mention a feature I'd like to see added, I've also thought of adding it myself (or trying to convince someone else to add it, or raising money to pay someone to add it). If I link to a bug that is closed in an issue tracker, it's because I have tested and, at the time of writing, I'm still experiencing the bug in an official/supported release that is supposed to have the fix.

Mobile usage is high for the users I support, so that was also a factor when I chose these services. Nextcloud, Jellyfin, and Wallabag have mobile apps and integrations, and I use these often.

The server-side commands for managing services are standardized: You'll see the pattern `dc SERVICE ACTION ARGS` repeated many times.

9.1. Nextcloud: file sync and share

A *Steadfast* personal cloud needs convenient file sharing and synchronization. Nextcloud is an excellent choice given its stability and popularity. It can be daunting to self-host, but mario makes it easy and fun.

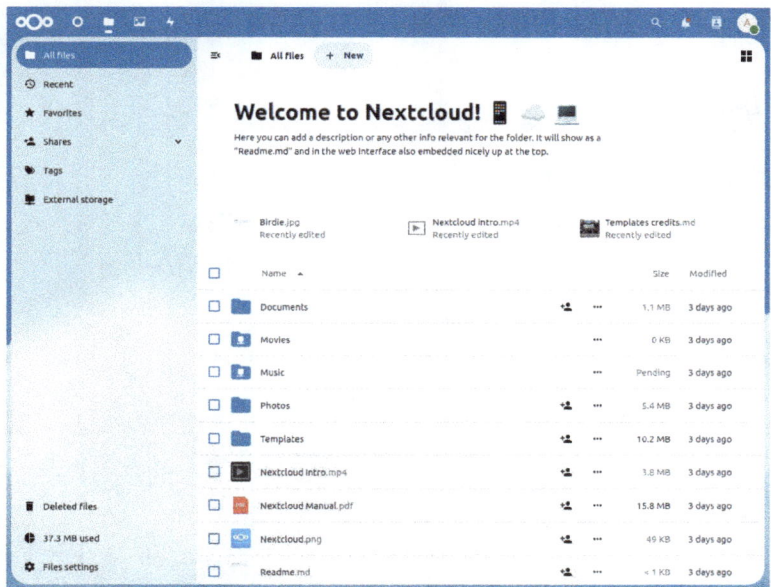

Figure 12. Nextcloud Files app screenshot showing files, folders, and share buttons.

A well-maintained Nextcloud server provides a solid foundation for de-Googling. Nextcloud can be self-hosted for free when installed via mario. Once you've got Nextcloud running, see Section 10.8, "More about Nextcloud" for lots of my opinions on how best to customize it.

9.1.1. Quick start

1. Provision with mario from your admin computer.
2. Start Nextcloud with `dc nextcloud up -d` on your server.
3. Navigate to `https://cloud.example.com` on your admin computer.

4. Follow the web-based setup page to create an admin account.
5. Skip installing recommended apps.

9.1.2. Maintenance notes

Run `dc nextcloud pull && dc nextcloud up -d` on your server to upgrade and replace Nextcloud service containers.

9.1.3. Issues

See Section 10.8.12, "Various issues".

9.2. Jellyfin: stream audio and video

Jellyfin [https://jellyfin.org] is a personal streaming media server. mario will set up a basic Jellyfin server.

Figure 13. Jellyfin screenshot showing metadata for a movie. Big Buck Bunny is licensed CC BY-3.0 by the Blender Foundation.

9.2.1. Quick start

1. Provision with mario from your admin computer.
2. Start Jellyfin with `dc jellyfin up -d` on your server.
3. Navigate to `https://jellyfin.example.com` on your admin computer.
4. Follow web-based setup steps.

If you have a GPU, look into hardware acceleration [https://jellyfin.org/docs/general/administration/hardware-acceleration/]. This is useful if videos can't be played directly by a client and need to be transcoded on the fly. Jellyfin can transcode using only CPU, but it is way faster with a GPU.

 Jellyfin can take advantage of some CPUs with built-in hardware transcoding. Intel Quick Sync Video, for instance.

9.2.2. Maintenance notes

Run `dc jellyfin pull && dc jellyfin up -d` on your server to upgrade and replace the Jellyfin service container.

9.2.3. Issues

Here are some features I'd love to see implemented in Jellyfin.

Feature: Share playlists

Playlists are private by design [https://github.com/jellyfin/jellyfin/issues/6264#issuecomment-1338518980]. I'd like the ability to share them [https://features.jellyfin.org/posts/173/share-playlists].

Feature: Clips

I often want to share, hear, or re-watch a specific part of some media. I think it would be just so cool to be able to create clips [https://features.jellyfin.org/posts/1036/bookmark-audio-video-segments] without actually creating new media files.

Feature: Offline mobile media

I want a Jellyfin mobile app that will automatically cache media and allow playing while offline [https://features.jellyfin.org/posts/218/support-offline-mode-on-android-mobile].

    Workaround: there are two separate mobile apps that can download and cache media for offline playing. Finamp [https://github.com/jmshrv/finamp] for music, and Findroid [https://github.com/jarnedemeulemeester/findroid] for video.

9.2.4. Manage Jellyfin media with Nextcloud

Jellyfin and Nextcloud both run on the same server. You can use this fact to leverage their individual strengths as services while they operate on the same data, one as the media streamer and one as the media file manager. mario creates special music and video folders on the server and makes them available to both services. Nextcloud "external storages" lets you upload files to these folders and Jellyfin will automatically notice and allow streaming the files you upload.

Nextcloud's `compose.yml` file has the entry `/data/shared/media/video:/data/video:rw` in `volumes`. `/data/shared/media/video` is the path on the server that will hold the actual video files, `/data/video` is where they'll show up inside the container, and `rw` says Nextcloud has read and write access to this volume. There's another similar folder for music files. See Section 10.8.4, "Detailed setup" for how to add them as external storages in Nextcloud.

In Jellyfin's `compose.yml` file you'll find similar lines to add music and videos volumes, but with `ro` (for read-only) instead of `rw`. Jellyfin only needs read access to the folders to be able to stream the files they contain.

To see the Nextcloud-managed media files in Jellyfin, add two media libraries:

1. Choose content type "Movies", click the "+" icon next to "Folders", and choose `/data/video`.

2. Choose content type "Music", click the "+" icon next to "Folders", and choose `/data/music`.

9.3. Wallabag: save and read articles

Wallabag [https://wallabag.org] saves articles for distraction-free offline reading.

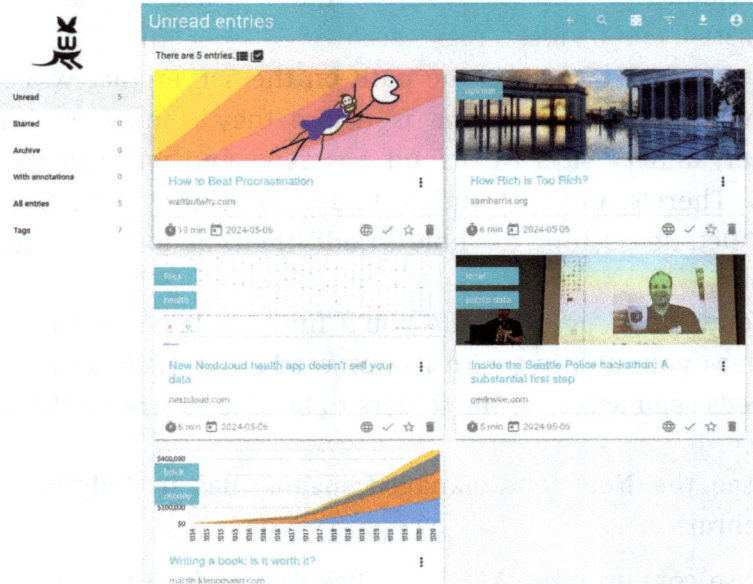

Figure 14. Wallabag screenshot showing unread articles view.

9.3.1. Quick start

1. Provision with mario from your admin computer.

2. Start Wallabag with `dc wallabag up -d` on your server.

3. Navigate to `https://wallabag.example.com` on your admin computer.

4. Log in as `wallabag` user with password `wallabag`.

5. Update password for `wallabag` user.

9.3.2. Maintenance notes

Run `dc wallabag pull && dc wallabag up -d` on your server to upgrade and replace Wallabag service containers. If you run into any issues, try manually applying database upgrades (see Section 9.3.3.1, "Bug:

Upgrades break everything"]).

9.3.3. Issues

Here's one issue I have with Wallabag and a feature I want.

Bug: Upgrades break everything

Database migrations are not (always?) automatically applied [https://github.com/wallabag/wallabag/issues/6649]. There may be other duplicate or related bug reports for this same thing, that's just one example. Luckily, there's an easy workaround [https://github.com/wallabag/docker#upgrading].

Apply the workaround to a mario system with:

Listing 29. force Wallabag database migration (🦖 server)

```
dc wallabag exec app /var/www/wallabag/bin/console \
  doctrine:migrations:migrate --env=prod --no-interaction
```

The `exec` command says we want to run something in a container. This runs the `console` utility in the `app` service container. The second line indicates necessary database migrations (schema and data updates) should be run using `prod` settings, without interactive prompts.

This is idempotent, as database migrations should be. After the first run, subsequent runs output: `[OK] Already at the latest version`.

It's unclear why thes migration is not automatically performed during an upgrade. Perhaps it is only necessary in special cases—I've only had to do it twice in a few years.

Feature: Share with other users

I want to be able to share content with other Wallabag users, within Wallabag [https://github.com/wallabag/wallabag/issues/679].

9.4. Watchtower: service updater

Watchtower is handy for keeping your Docker containers up to date. It will discover and check outdated containers, pull new images, and restart services to create new containers.

If you never want containers upgrading automatically, don't run Watchtower. Or, use configuration settings [https://containrrr.dev/watchtower/arguments/] to allow or block auto-upgrades for particular containers. mario uses a container label to prevent watchtower from updating Scratch, for example.

9.4.1. Quick start

1. Provision with mario from your admin computer.
2. Start Watchtower with `dc watchtower up -d` on your server.

From now on it'll run in the background, automatically upgrading containers whenever possible, on a reasonable schedule (every 24 hours by default). You can forget about it until it breaks (or breaks something else).

9.4.2. Maintenance notes

Run `dc watchtower pull && dc watchtower up -d` on your server to upgrade and replace the Watchtower service container.

9.4.3. Issues

It [does not automatically roll back if a container upgrade fails](https://github.com/containrrr/watchtower/issues/90). Granted, this would be challenging to implement. A service might only have one-way database migrations, for example. I think the Watchtower maintainers made the right decision to omit automatic rollbacks (likely to keep Watchtower simple).

You may experience an issue where a service is broken by Watchtower. If you suspect this is the case and you know when the service started breaking, try to correlate that with any upgrades appearing in `dc watchtower logs`. I avoid this by only using Watchtower for non-critical services. I don't let Watchtower auto-upgrade my Nextcloud service, for example.

9.5. Scratch: visual programming

Scratch is a popular and very approachable visual programming language geared towards interactive multimedia and learning. The most well-known public online version [https://scratch.mit.edu] adds sharing, studios, comments, stars, hearts, endless memes and games. These "social" features may be exactly what a user wants/needs (e.g. one may remix an existing project and learn from it), or it may unintentionally reorient a user from productive creation to mindless consumption (e.g. doomscrolling).

This is where your new *Steadfast* power comes in: Scratch can be self-hosted without the social features. In fact, that's the simplest way to self-host it. This is a great option if your users want to focus on creating in Scratch and being social in person. 😊

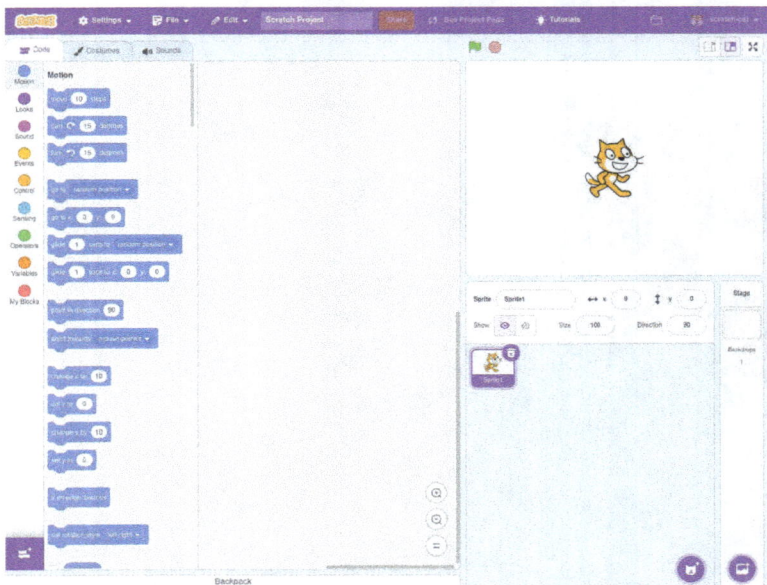

Figure 15. Scratch screenshot showing a new empty project.

Scratch doesn't require any persistent data, setup, nor auth.

9.5.1. Quick start

1. Provision with mario from your admin computer.
2. Start Scratch with `dc scratch up -d` on your server.
3. Navigate to https://scratch.example.com on your admin computer.

9.5.2. Maintenance notes

Scratch uses a custom Docker image so the upgrade process is significantly more complex than upgrading other services. First, open the Scratch `custom/Dockerfile` on your admin computer. That `Dockerfile` can be found in a subfolder of `mario/ansible` in the mario source code.

If you want to base the image on a newer version of Node.js, visit the [Node.js page on Docker Hub](https://hub.docker.com/_/node) [https://hub.docker.com/_/node] and select a version to use in the `FROM` line of the `Dockerfile`. If you want to upgrade Scratch, visit the [releases page](https://github.com/scratchfoundation/scratch-gui/releases) [https://github.com/scratchfoundation/scratch-gui/releases] and select a version to use for `SCRATCH_VERSION` in the `Dockerfile`.

Re-run `provision.sh` on the admin computer. Re-build the image with `dc scratch build --pull` on the server. Finally, replace the Scratch service container by running `dc scratch up -d` on the server.

100   Steadfast Self-Hosting

10. What's next?

By this point, I'm assuming you've got your server running and some services too. Here's where you can find a handful of ideas for what to try next.

10.1. Learn more

If you like this book, and you want to learn and do more, do it. Ride that wave of inspiration. Seek both breadth and depth.

For breadth, look for a comprehensive book about Linux since mario expects Linux, and a better understanding of Linux can help you customize your server with confidence. There aren't any Ubuntu-specific dependencies, but Ubuntu is the only Linux flavor mario has been extensively tested on at the time of writing. One of my first purchases when I wanted to just finally "get" Linux was *UNIX: The Complete Reference*, a thousand-page monster covering many, many concepts. I studied it in chunks, referred to it often, and never read it cover to cover. If I started learning again from scratch today, I'd still have a book like that handy while studying online resources and trying stuff at home.

For depth, immerse yourself in fundamentals. Learn how a computer works. Push past abstractions and make progress towards first principles. Take a computer science class in an area supporting something else you want to do. For example, if you want to code your own web services, take a class in programming for the web. If you want to understand how source code makes a computer do things, take a class in compilers.

Work through this book in a class or small group. See Chapter 12, *Discussion topics* and Chapter 13, *Exercises*.

Participate in FOSS communities to learn from and share with others. Pass on what you've learned. File a bug. Post in a forum. It's fun!

Conferences like SeaGL [https://seagl.org] bring together bright minds on many topics, including self-hosting. If you've done something cool, share it!

10.2. Use a GPU

A GPU offers more efficient video transcoding with Jellyfin, reducing server CPU usage and speeding up remote video streaming.

A FOSS voice assistant would benefit from a GPU.

A GPU could also speed up video transcoding and facial recognition.

Modern generative AI workloads like large language model chat and image generation are much faster with a GPU.

10.3. AI

AI is once again the latest hotness. You can run your own image generators and LLMs (large-language models) at home. No GPU is required. Here's a `compose.yml` that'll work with mario to stand up LocalAI [https://localai.io].

Listing 30. example LocalAI service config

```yaml
version: '3.6'

services:
  api:
    image: quay.io/go-skynet/local-ai:latest
```

```yaml
      environment:
        MODELS_PATH: /models
      volumes:
        - /data/localai/models:/models:cached
      command: ["/usr/bin/local-ai"]
      labels:
        - "traefik.enable=true"
        - "traefik.http.routers.localai-https.entrypoints=websecure"
        - "traefik.http.routers.localai-https.rule=Host(`localai.example.com`)"
        - "traefik.http.routers.localai-https.tls.certresolver=myresolver"
        - "traefik.http.routers.localai-https.middlewares=lan-only"
      networks:
        - traefik_default
      restart: unless-stopped
networks:
  traefik_default:
    external: true
```

Note the middleware to only allow traffic from your LAN. This assumes your LAN uses 192.168.1.* addresses, and expects a corresponding label on the Traefik container to set up the middleware, for example:

Listing 31. label from Traefik configuration allowing only LAN access

```
"traefik.http.middlewares.lan-only.ipallowlist.sourcerange=192.168.1.0/24"
```

 Use mario to provision your LocalAI service.

See the LocalAI documentation [https://localai.io] for further setup help. Once you get that running, you can use the Nextcloud AI integration app [https://apps.nextcloud.com/apps/integration_openai] as a convenient frontend.

10.4. Pi-hole

Running a Pi-hole [https://pi-hole.net] service in your LAN helps block advertisements, trackers, and bad actors using DNS block lists.

Clients (laptops, phones, etc) on your network use the Pi-hole as their DNS server, generally as part of DHCP (Dynamic Host Configuration Protocol) auto-configuration by your router or Pi-hole itself (if you use Pi-hole as your DHCP server).

The Pi-hole translates domain names to IP addresses. If a domain name is on a block list, it returns a false IP address such as 0.0.0.0.

The technique is imperfect, yet simple and effective.

My Pi-hole server sits between my router's DNS server and all clients.

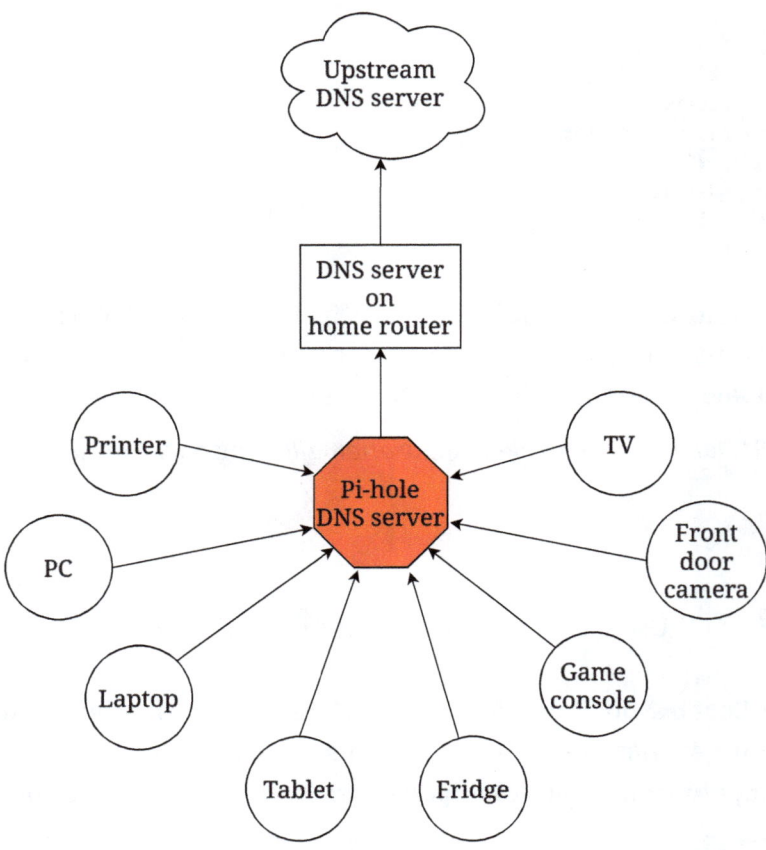

Figure 16. Pi-hole DNS traffic flow diagram.

Queries for domain names not on any block list will be answered directly or sent upstream. I set up my Pi-hole to pass queries on to my home router, which will then query a DNS server outside my LAN as necessary.

It's easy to block individual domain names or entire lists as you see fit. I've used this as an "impulse blocker", helping the kids avoid distractions during remote school.

The Pi-Hole also has a list of local DNS entries. I add a few domain names to this list for servers inside my LAN.

Note that some clients will by default bypass an auto-configured DNS server such as Pi-hole. For example, DNS over HTTPS in Firefox [https://support.mozilla.org/kb/firefox-dns-over-https].

10.5. Single sign-on

It would be convenient for users to be able to log in once to get access to all self-hosted services using a common, consistent, and well-designed mechanism (single sign-on), and for sysadmins to be able to manage all users and groups in one place (centralized identity management).

Authentik [https://goauthentik.io] is one service providing this, and appears to have all the features I want (single sign-on, backend user database, integrates with everything I self-host). I want to try it out and see it running well for a good while before adding it to mario. Some of the other self-hosting solutions mentioned in Section 11.2, "Alternatives to mario" do include FOSS central identity management.

10.6. Enforce SSH public key auth

Some sysadmins choose to require public key authentication for SSH logins. I think it's a good idea [https://security.stackexchange.com/q/3887] but I didn't want to force it on you so I didn't include it in mario. I'm using this as an opportunity to demonstrate how to extend mario. Add this Ansible task to `roles/base/tasks/main.yml`:

Listing 32. enforce SSH public key auth (🏠 admin computer)

```
# This does not affect logging in from a console (e.g. directly connected
# keyboard and monitor, or a virtual console).
- name: Disable tunneled clear text passwords
  copy:
    src: pka-only.conf
    dest: /etc/ssh/sshd_config.d/
```

```
      owner: root
      group: root
      mode: 0400
    notify:
      - restart sshd
```

Add this to `roles/base/handlers/main.yml`:

Listing 33. Ansible handler to restart SSH (🏠 admin computer)

```
- name: restart sshd
  service:
    name: sshd.service
    state: restarted
```

Create `roles/base/files/pka-only.conf` with:

Listing 34. SSH server config lines (🏠 admin computer)

```
PasswordAuthentication no
AuthenticationMethods publickey
```

Finally, re-run `provision.sh`. From now on, your server will require public key authentication for SSH logins.

10.7. Allow WAN access

mario blocks WAN access by default. Read Section 6.2, "Digital security" to decide if you want this or not. You may remove this protection by removing the `lan-only` middleware from the corresponding router's Traefik label. For example, to allow WAN access to Nextcloud, make this change in Traefik's `compose.yml`:

Listing 35. patch for WAN access to Nextcloud (🏠 admin computer)

```
- traefik.http.routers.nc-https.middlewares=nc-head,nc-redir,lan-only
+ traefik.http.routers.nc-https.middlewares=nc-head,nc-redir
```

Similarly for Jellyfin, you may delete the whole line referencing the `lan-only` middleware in Jellyfin's `compose.yml` if you decide to expose that service on your WAN.

10.8. More about Nextcloud

Nextcloud is a key part of my self-hosting setup. I wanted to include a lot of additional details without cluttering up Chapter 9, *Services*, so you'll find these extra sections here.

10.8.1. Basic install

A basic (default, un-customized) Nextcloud install provides remote file storage, organization, and sharing. It keeps track of actual files and folders stored somewhere (local, remote, cloud, wherever) and tracks additional metadata about those files and folders in a database. You access it via a web browser and there is a desktop client to sync files locally, similar to Dropbox, Google Drive, and OneDrive.

I've come to *really* trust file sync with the Nextcloud desktop app. If I see a check mark on my desktop app, I know everything is properly synchronized with the server. I am constantly creating and editing content locally and counting on sync to work (usually on my desktop computer), or creating and editing directly in Nextcloud via the web UI.

There are also apps for mobile devices. I'll come back to mobile later in the following sections.

10.8.2. Object storage

Nextcloud is able to use object storage for primary data storage. This is an advanced topic left as an exercise to the reader. I'll assume primary storage on a local HDD set up by mario.

10.8.3. Security

A basic Nextcloud install appears to have excellent security. The source is in heavy use and is backed by a solid company with a reputation that depends on their commitment to security. They make it easy to lock down and vet (it is FOSS after all). The defaults appear secure. They follow best practices. They have a public bounty program and threat model.

10.8.4. Detailed setup

To confirm reproducibility of your Nextcloud server, destroy and re-create it (before you use it for real). After you get it working once, stop it with `dc nextcloud down`. Destroy all persistent data with `sudo rm -rf /data/nextcloud`. That *really* deletes everything. Re-provision with mario (run `provision.sh` again). Follow the setup steps again, see Section 9.1.1, "Quick start".

Read the official docs at `/settings/help` or docs.nextcloud.com.

Add apps at `/settings/apps`. See Section 10.8.7, "Customization" for tips on how to roll out apps thoughtfully and which ones are worth your time.

Test configuring a mail server and sending an email at `/settings/admin` (Basic settings).

Add users at `/settings/users`.

Check logs for all containers related to Netcloud with `dc nextcloud logs -f`.

Check Nextcloud internal logs at `/settings/admin/logging` in the web UI or `/data/nextcloud/root/data/nextcloud.log` on the server. These include specific Nextcloud internal server messages and are often more useful to me than the container logs. If you see a warning about "1 error in the logs since DATE" (or perhaps a couple) at `/settings/admin/logging`, you can probably ignore it. These initial logged errors appear to be harmless, possibly a result of some install-time race conditions. It is still a good idea to review all logged errors.

Review "Security & setup warnings" at `/settings/admin/overview`. You can ignore the warning "Could not check for JavaScript support. Please check manually if your webserver serves `.mjs` files using the JavaScript MIME type." if this succeeds on your admin computer:

Listing 36. JavaScript fetch test (🏠 admin computer)

```
curl -I https://cloud.example.com/apps/settings/js/esm-test.mjs
```

The warning is because the Nextcloud `app` container [fails at a test](https://github.com/nextcloud/server/issues/42989) to request a JavaScript test file, likely because of a DNS issue. To fix it, the request must be able to work from within the Nextcloud `app` container. In other words, this must succeed (return a successful HTTP response code and include the header `content-type: text/javascript`):

Listing 37. JavaScript fetch test (🐦 server)

```
dc nextcloud exec app \
    curl -I https://cloud.example.com/apps/settings/js/esm-test.mjs
```

Some maintenance requires the `occ` tool (short for "ownCloud command"). Run it with `dc nextcloud exec --user www-data app php occ`.

Add `/data/video` as an External storage. Media files uploaded there will automatically appear in Jellyfin. First, visit `/settings/apps/featured` and install the "External storage support" app. Next, visit `/settings/admin/externalstorages` and install the "External storage support" app.

- Folder name: Video
- External storage: Local
- Authentication: None
- Configuration: `/data/video`
- Set users, previews, sharing, and remaining options as desired.

Add `/data/music` as an External storage, similar to `/data/video`.

10.8.5. More maintenance tips

Visit `/settings/admin/overview` periodically to check for system and security issues that may require manual intervention. Perform any recommended maintenance on that page. Ignore the Update section, it may disagree with Docker Hub. Visit `/settings/admin/logging` periodically to review all server-side log messages.

Running `dc nextcloud pull && dc nextcloud up -d` (on the server) will pull the most recent image of github.com/nextcloud/docker with the `stable` release tag. Using this tag will likely be stable enough for you and your users. `stable` generally corresponds to the version they call *previous* at docs.nextcloud.com/.

You may opt to "pin" your Nextcloud to a more specific tag such as `27.1.5-apache`. This gives you the chance to review and test each upgrade. You can pin a release tag in Nextcloud's `compose.yml` where the image name appears, just trade `stable` for the tag you choose. All available tags are listed at Docker Hub [https://hub.docker.com/_/nextcloud].

> Nextcloud's blog posts and marketing materials use different version names than the release versions from source control. "Hub 6" on the blog refers to versions `27._._` in source control, "Hub 7" to `28._._`, and so on.

Release cadence

A major release is shipped every four months [https://docs.nextcloud.com/server/stable/admin_manual/release_schedule.html]. The Nextcloud apps I care about seem to keep up with this pace, but it does feel a bit aggressive to me. Developers need to modify their apps each time at least slightly, or heavily if breaking API changes occur. Thankfully the Nextcloud team carefully documents changes [https://help.nextcloud.com/t/new-process-for-documenting-core-code-changes-that-affect-app-developers/149828/1] to ease app maintenance for developers.

As a *Steadfast* sysadmin, be sure to check your `/settings/admin/overview` page before upgrading Nextcloud to make sure all the apps you use will work with the version you're upgrading to. You can override an out-of-date app with the "enable untested app" option under `/settings/apps`. Sometimes this works.

Since four months seemed to me like a short window for major releases I started a thread about it [https://help.nextcloud.com/t/major-release-cadence/161685]. Review their Maintenance and Release Schedule [https://github.com/nextcloud/server/wiki/Maintenance-and-Release-Schedule] to make sure your current version is still supported.

10.8.6. Performance

If you use mario to deploy Nextcloud, you'll start with a nominally performant server suitable for a small handful of users, assuming you have sufficient hardware resources. mario includes an author-approved selection of the recommended server tuning steps [https://docs.nextcloud.com/server/stable/admin_manual/installation/server_tuning.html].

I've only had one performance issue in the years I've hosted Nextcloud (knock wood!), so I'll mention it here. I was seeing slow web requests along with lots of database activity [https://github.com/nextcloud/server/issues/35311]. This had me under the hood with MariaDB for a while. They've since fixed the root cause [https://github.com/nextcloud/server/pull/33540] so it isn't a problem for new installations.

10.8.7. Customization

Nextcloud can be used as-is (see Section 10.8.1, "Basic install") or heavily customized. The simplest and safest way to customize is by installing an app from the built-in app store (`/settings/apps`), especially if an app is marked "featured". These *Nextcloud apps* are installed on the server, expanding the functionality of a base Nextcloud instance.

Here are some Nextcloud apps I've tried, what they do, and a ruling on whether they're worth looking into. Read "Worth your time?" as "Adam maybe tried this app and has shared his opinion whether others will find this particular app worth the effort to learn and maintain, based on his own experiences projected onto our possibly different use cases." Grain of salt, in other words. When in doubt, start small (default Nextcloud install), and roll these out thoughtfully if you do at all.

Table 4. Nextcloud apps commentary

Nextcloud App	Purpose	Worth your time?
Antivirus for files	virus scan uploads	**Yes**. Note: uploads from desktop clients are not scanned for viruses [https://github.com/nextcloud/files_antivirus/issues/219].
Analytics	track and graph metrics	**Yes**. Only for small/simple use cases though.
Appointments	easy 3rd party scheduling	**Yes**. Requires careful calendar curation. Somewhat fiddly setup.
Calendar	manage meetings and appointments	**Yes**. See also: Section 10.8.12.7, "Spurious event updated notifications".
Circles	arbitrarily group users	**No opinion**. I don't have enough users to justify this.
Collectives	wiki or knowledge base	**Maybe**. Looks like a useful way to organize a set of related documents. Requires Circles.
Cookbook	recipe manager	**Yes**. Great at importing from web pages (thanks to standardized recipe data already present in HTML source). I wish it were better at printing/exporting though.
Contacts	address book	**Yes**.
Dashboard	landing page	**No**. I like to go right to my files.
Deck	kanban board	**No opinion**. I tried it a little and it worked, I just don't use kanban much.
Draw.io	diagram editor	**Yes**.

Nextcloud App	Purpose	Worth your time?
Duplicate Finder	find and cull duplicate files	**No**. Slow and opaque. I recommend rdfind [https://github.com/pauldreik/rdfind] instead.
Electronic Signatures	e-sign documents	**No**. Requires a 3rd party service. I'd rather have drawn signatures. See Section 10.8.12.5, "Draw signature in forms".
End-to-End Encryption	encrypt files server-side, decrypt with client	**No**. Unnervingly buggy. Confusing UI/UX. See Section 10.8.13, "End-to-End Encryption".
Files	file management, sharing	**Yes**, although the "Versions" tab is not very useful.
Forms	Google Forms alternative	**Yes**.
Full text search	search through all documents	**Maybe**. Fast. Buggy. Likely dormant project. See Section 10.8.8, "Full text search".
Holiday Calendars	easily add public holiday calendars	**Yes**. The configuration for this app shows up under "Personal" → "Availability" for me, not "Groupware" (although the URL path is `/settings/user/groupware`).
Maps	maps and directions	**Yes**. Grab a cup of tea if you have lots of photos with GPS coordinate metadata.

Nextcloud App	Purpose	Worth your time?
Mail	email	**No opinion**. I tried it briefly and it choked on my bazillion Gmail messages. And yes, I do want to de-Gmail someday.
Memories	photos	**Yes**. Requires Photos.
News	track blogs and news via rss/atom feeds	**Yes**.
Nextcloud Office	edit spreadsheets, slides, etc.	**Yes**. I don't love this but I need it. Maybe that's a "No"? Mobile apps for this are painful. See Section 10.8.11, "Nextcloud Office".
Notes	simple markdown-based note taking	**Yes**. There's an excellent companion mobile app. Replaced Google Notes for me.
Passwords	password manager	**Yes**. Warning: online only (requires connection to Nextcloud server).
PhoneTrack	location sharing and tracking	**Yes**. UI is feature-rich and complicated. Traveled movement lines are cool.
Photos	photos, sorta	**No**. Slow, clumsy, lacking features compared with other FOSS photo management software. Use Memories instead. Note that Memories depends on the Photos app.
Polls	simple polls	**Yes**.

Nextcloud App	Purpose	Worth your time?
Ransomware protection	warns for bad file names on upload	**No**. Too many false positives. Unmaintained.
Recognize	face recognition	**No**.
Suspicious login	warn about suspicious IPs	**No**. Too many false positives.
Tasks	tasks/todos	**Yes**.
Tables	tabular data entry and API	**No**. Not yet, although keep an eye on this as a potentially powerful and useful low-code platform.
Talk	video and text chat	**No**. Works, just not as well as other video and text chat services/apps. I do use it for my chicken safety system and I see it improving a lot with each release. For now I recommend Signal [https://signal.org] instead.
Temporary files lock	avoid edit conflicts	**Yes**.
Text	edit text documents	**Yes**. I'm a huge fan of Markdown plain text documents, and Nextcloud handles these well. It has a nice web-based collaborative editor. I like pasting in rich text and letting the editor auto-convert it to Markdown. See also: Section 10.8.12.2, "Mobile text editing is hard" and Section 10.8.12.4, "Spurious web text editor conflicts".

Nextcloud App	Purpose	Worth your time?
Video converter	transcode videos	**No.** Cool idea but the project appears dormant.

10.8.8. Full text search

This app allows you to search through all content of all documents on your server. The search syntax is hard to get right. It uses a lot of CPU [https://github.com/nextcloud/fulltextsearch/issues/601] and is memory-hungry too.

The GitHub project repositories are pretty quiet. See:

- github.com/nextcloud/fulltextsearch/pulse
- github.com/nextcloud/files_fulltextsearch/pulse
- github.com/nextcloud/fulltextsearch_elasticsearch/pulse

10.8.9. Mobile

Nextcloud works OK as the backend for a mobile device. It can be your single reliable source of truth for contacts, calendars, tasks, and most everything else that matters on mobile. You can open files and edit them, but the UI/UX is bad. See Section 10.8.12.2, "Mobile text editing is hard" for a couple workarounds.

Besides the primary mobile app (called simply "Nextcloud"), there are other mobile apps made to work with Nextcloud apps. Here are the ones I recommend. I don't have an iPhone so these are only Android apps.

Table 5. Recommended Nextcloud mobile apps

Mobile app	Works with Nextcloud apps	More info
DAVx5	Calendar, Contacts, Tasks	davx5.com

Mobile app	Works with Nextcloud apps	More info
Maps Geofavorites	Maps	github.com/penguin86/nextcloud-maps-client
NC Passwords	Passwords	gitlab.com/joleaf/nc-passwords-app
Nextcloud Cookbook	Cookbook	github.com/nextcloud/cookbook
Notes	Files, Notes, Text	github.com/nextcloud/notes-android
OpenTasks	Tasks	github.com/dmfs/opentasks
Nextcloud Talk	Talk	apps.nextcloud.com/apps/spreed

Android devices usually ship with groupware (calendar and contacts) apps, or you can install your favorite ones. DAVx5 handles synchronization of groupware data to and from your device. DAVx5 is only necessary on Android, perhaps because iOS has better native WebDAV support. DAVx5 is not needed on Murena phones (/e/ OS).

There are actually two Cookbook apps. Either works fine for me. I'm not picky, I just need to see the ingredients and directions. Looks like the one by "Teifun2" is more popular.

Maps Geofavorites lets you easily save arbitrary GPS coordinates to the Maps Nextcloud app. Handy for remembering where you parked your bike, for example.

Notes looks best configured in Grid View.

Talk... despite my own advice, I find myself using Talk anyway. I like having my own chat server, I guess. I am listing it here because I do actually use it, and to complain that I can't read messages offline [https://github.com/nextcloud/talk-android/issues/217]. It is also under heavy development and improving lots with every release.

These are just a few examples. Since you've got all your data and Nextcloud always uses open formats, you can ride the wave of improvements and enjoy what works best. For example, I just started using RunnerUp [https://github.com/jonasoreland/runnerup]. When I save my tracks in Nextcloud, they automatically show up in Maps. Nice!

10.8.10. Nextcloud vs. ownCloud

At first glance it's a bit difficult to tell the difference between Nextcloud and ownCloud. This follows since Nextcloud started as a fork of ownCloud.

So why should you choose one over the other? A healthy FOSS project is generally also an active project, so one way to guide your decision is by comparing activity metrics on GitHub. See owncloud/core activity [https://github.com/owncloud/core/pulse] and nextcloud/server activity [https://github.com/nextcloud/server/pulse]. Based on those two sets of metrics it appears Nextcloud is thriving and ownCloud is dying.

Another interpretation is that ownCloud has a smaller and slower-moving core codebase. More work is necessary to make a truly rigorous comparison.

See also: Traits of Good Self-Hosted Services and Traits of Bad Self-Hosted Services in Section 7.1.1, "Choose services".

10.8.11. Nextcloud Office

nextcloud.com/office/ gives some strong hints how the company behind Nextcloud wants us to think of "office" and their plans for it as a suite of related tools. They clearly intend a holistic, integrated office experience, and Nextcloud can be configured to be used in this manner. nextcloud.com/office/ covers editing office documents (rich text and spreadsheets) collaboratively, along with uses for the Notes, Collectives, and Tables apps. It provides some clever and useful workflow ideas.

Given that wide a scope, groupware should be part of "office" too, so instead let's for now focus specifically on collaborative editing of office documents. Doing this within Nextcloud requires an app called Nextcloud Office [https://apps.nextcloud.com/apps/richdocuments] as well as a separate backend service, either Collabora or ONLYOFFICE. My strong preference is for Collabora, in line with Section 7.1.1.1, "Good for self-hosting"; despite fewer stars on GitHub, it appears Collabora development is flourishing while ONLYOFFICE is stagnant (although it's hard to tell which of the many ONLYOFFICE repositories on GitHub are relevant here).

10.8.12. Various issues

Here's a selection of my favorite bugs and feature requests for Nextcloud.

Spinner on mobile

When you first open the Nextcloud mobile app, a loading spinner shows up in front of a cached view of whatever files and folders existed the last time you use the app. If you ignore it and tap to navigate your way into a folder or open a file, you may end up tapping a different one than you intended because the folder order can change *as you are tapping the screen*.
 Workarounds:

- wait until the spinner completes (usually takes me about one second)
- reduce chance of reordering with "A - Z" or "Z - A" sorting instead of "Newest first" or "Oldest first"

Mobile text editing is hard

Nextcloud makes it easy to get to your stuff via mobile devices, but editing is a pain.
 This is not a Nextcloud-only problem; I find *all* mobile text entry and editing cumbersome. This applies to email, plain text, Markdown, and office documents.
 In Nextcloud-land, one workaround to improve plain and Markdown text entry is to use the Notes app on Android [https://github.com/nextcloud/notes-android] or iOS [https://github.com/nextcloud/notes-ios]. It has separate editing and viewing modes and more

aggressive synchronization. With Notes you have a better chance of up-to-date data and fewer conflicts.

Another workaround is to use Markor [https://github.com/gsantner/markor]. Install that app, then:

1. In the Nextcloud mobile app, "Download" or "Sync" the file you wish to view or edit locally. This caches a copy on your phone.
2. In the Nextcloud mobile app, choose "open with" for the file. Should open instantly.
3. If you make changes to the file, save it, then manually "Sync" the file in the Nextcloud app. It appears local changes like these never make it to the server otherwise.

See jenson.org/text/ for background on why mobile text editing is a complex and multifaceted problem.

Cumbersome mobile setup

To sync calendars, tasks, and contacts with your phone's storage of same on Android, you must install and configure the 3rd party DAVx5 app. I don't know why DAVx5 is required [https://help.nextcloud.com/t/what-does-android-file-sync-do-for-a-nextcloud-account/154330], but Murena [https://murena.com] figured it out for me. Their Android-derived /e/ OS includes native support for Nextcloud accounts, removing the requirement for DAVx5. Users with iOS and other OSes besides Android can sync groupware-related data without DAVx5 [https://docs.nextcloud.com/server/stable/user_manual/en/groupware/].

Spurious web text editor conflicts

Collaborating on plain text and Markdown text files sometimes results in spurious conflicts. Editing is interrupted before it starts, and the web-based text file editor shows you two versions of the file side by side. The left side is labeled "Use current version", and the right says "Use the saved version" (or equivalents for your locale or specific client).

Apparently the browser has a saved copy in local storage or something that gets loaded first and considers it the "current" version. Then it loads the one on the right and calls it the "saved" version, and if they differ you get to choose.

Workaround: pick the one on the right. That's the latest and greatest copy as it exists server-side.

Why the... never mind, just pick the one on the right. If you're curious and want to dig in deeper, follow these links:

- Shared text file is not up-to-date with saved file [https://github.com/nextcloud/text/issues/2388]

- Changing File from Desktop leads to conflict in browser, even if browser was not doing any changes [https://github.com/nextcloud/text/issues/4078]

- Text: document current vs. saved version [https://help.nextcloud.com/t/text-document-current-vs-saved-version/151600] (by yours truly)

Related desktop client bug: Nextcloud-Client creating conflicts when it should not [https://github.com/nextcloud/desktop/issues/2467]. Conflicts seem to appear in cases where there shouldn't be any. Workarounds: wait 10 seconds or so between saves until the desktop client syncs and returns to idle (roll your eyes while you wait). Also, check out the Temporary files lock [https://apps.nextcloud.com/apps/files_lock] app for semi-automated advisory locking (e.g. quickly communicate "gimme a minute, I'm editing that Markdown text file").

Draw signature in forms

Forms are handy for gathering simple minimally-structured data... surveys, RSVPs, stuff like that. The data are just dumped into a spreadsheet. With a signature field Forms could be used to add a drawn signature to a form like a contract or waiver.

There are extant Nextcloud online signature apps that incorporate digital signatures [https://en.wikipedia.org/wiki/Digital_signature]. I don't want or need digital signatures, especially since they appear to rely on 3rd party services. I really just want a low-tech image that looks like a drawn signature at the bottom of a page. It doesn't even need to be wet ink. If you want that too, vote for or help with github.com/nextcloud/forms/issues/947.

OpenSign [https://github.com/OpenSignLabs/OpenSign] and DocuSeal [https://github.com/docusealco/docuseal] are two alternative FOSS self-hostable apps supporting drawn signatures.

Release script missing from source

Nextcloud is FOSS, although some release scripts are held back [https://help.nextcloud.com/t/build-bzip-and-package-from-git/58341]. They may or may not be required to release those, I don't know. I hope they do decide to release them, for the same reasons the rest of Nextcloud is FOSS.

Spurious event updated notifications

The Calendar app is quite useful and perhaps the most heavily used by me and my users. I have grown to expect one particular erroneous "event updated" notifications, possibly caused by calendar client/sync issues.

On one shared calendar (with many clients) I often get notifications that so-and-so "updated event XYZ in calendar ABC", but the only actual thing that occurred is that one of the clients just sync'd (or perhaps made some innocuous change to an event) and Nextcloud thinks it was a meaningful update [https://github.com/nextcloud/calendar/issues/5879]. At least, I think that's what's happening... some changes (like changing the event's date) do show up with the old and new values made explicit. As an aside, I do like this "explicit diff" behavior showing the exact changes made to an event's Title, Time, Location, or Description.

10.8.13. End-to-End Encryption

End-to-End encrypted folders seems like a great idea. There's a Nextcloud app for this and I recommend you avoid it.

It seems close to working, but it feels like early-release software.

The UI/UX is confusing, and I ran into a dealbreaker bug that left files decrypted server-side. Furthermore, [sharing](https://help.nextcloud.com/t/how-to-setup-e2e-encryption-for-shared-folders/165610) [doesn't work](https://help.nextcloud.com/t/e2ee-and-file-sharing/145547) [https://github.com/nextcloud/end_to_end_encryption/issues/520], [there's no web client](https://github.com/nextcloud/end_to_end_encryption/issues/82), [the roadmap is unclear](https://github.com/nextcloud/end_to_end_encryption/issues/285), and [keys are always stored on the server](https://github.com/nextcloud/end_to_end_encryption/issues/8) (these are thankfully stored encrypted).

Sorry for all those really long links. Whew! Deep breaths, self, deep breaths. Count to ten.

Proceed carefully with the End-to-End Encryption Nextcloud app. Review [known issues](https://github.com/nextcloud/end_to_end_encryption/issues), make sure you can live with all those, then test it out thoroughly using a throwaway/sandbox Nextcloud instance. Make sure it works with all clients you plan to use it with (e.g. desktop, mobile).

10.8.14. AIO installer

Among the myriad Nextcloud install methods, there's a relatively new and interesting AIO ("all-in-one") installer (nextcloud.com/all-in-one). It's free for an instance with less than 100 users. The AIO takes a different approach than mario, it configures and manages multiple Nextcloud-related service containers for you. I recommend the mario method instead for its flexible and empowering experience of learning how to add and manage individual containers yourself.

See the [AIO readme](https://github.com/nextcloud/all-in-one) for more information.

11. More resources

Visit selfhostbook.com for all supporting material including source code for this book and mario.

- Source code [https://selfhostbook.com/code/]
- Contact information [https://selfhostbook.com/contact/]

Patches and feedback are most welcome. This book is just a part of something big and I'm glad you're a part of it too!

11.1. Support

Here are a few ideas for when you get stuck.

- Ask for help in forums and chats related to a product/project.
- If you're confident you've found a bug, file an issue with the product/project.
- Ask other readers [https://selfhostbook.com/chat/] for help.
- Try your luck in semi-moderated public places. Don't expect much from these, although you may get lucky from time to time.
    - selfhosted subreddit [https://reddit.com/r/selfhosted/]

- [homelab subreddit](https://reddit.com/r/homelab/) [https://reddit.com/r/homelab/]
    - [Nextcloud chat](https://matrix.to/#/#Nextcloud:matrix.org) [https://matrix.to/#/#Nextcloud:matrix.org]
    - [self-hosted chat](https://matrix.to/#/#selfhosted:matrix.org) [https://matrix.to/#/#selfhosted:matrix.org]
- Hire me to help you out.

11.2. Alternatives to mario

If you're in a hurry, you can find one-click-install appliances with many ready-to-go apps. FreedomBox [https://freedombox.org] is one promising contender in this space.

There are also many shortcuts and frontends for self-hosting. For example, openmediavault [https://openmediavault.org] looks like a cool way to build a DIY (do it yourself) NAS (network attached storage).

And there are countless more of these kinds of partial or full-service self-hosting solutions, such as:

YunoHost [https://yunohost.org]

Not considered, I prefer always using containers.

CasaOS [https://casaos.io]

New, interesting, very little documentation.

Runtipi [https://runtipi.io]

New, interesting, uses Docker Compose and Traefik.

These look intriguing, and it's hopeful (and overwhelming) to see many options in this space. I evaluated these only just enough to get the sense they didn't fit my wants and needs. I'm a crotchety old man and I'm reluctant to change, but I still do, sometimes. If and when I adopt something new, it must pass a high bar, ideally most or all these tests:

> ### Checklist: Self-Hosting Solution Viability
>
> - ☐ Will it work for years with minimal tinkering?
> - ☐ Is it easily extensible?

- ☐ Do I trust the maintainers?
- ☐ Does it employ technologies I'm familiar with?
- ☐ Does it weaken or strengthen security by changing my attack surface?
- ☐ Does it add features/value I need/want, beyond what I'm already able to do?
- ☐ Will it help my users?
- ☐ Will it help me learn what I need/want to learn, and safely take care of the rest for me without my needing to learn more?
- ☐ Will it help me figure out why I made a change to one of my services two years ago?
- ☐ Does it phone home, using telemetry or my data in a way I don't approve?
- ☐ Does it hold back "enterprise" features I need, even for my scaled-down use case? Is it annoying about this, reminding me often?
- ☐ If I want paid support, is it available?
- ☐ Is it popular? Has it been around a while, and do I expect it to endure?

See also: Traits of Good Self-Hosted Services and Traits of Bad Self-Hosted Services in Section 7.1.1, "Choose services".

After brief reviews, I find existing self-hosting solutions generally:

- are new and immature
- lack proper documentation
- do too much: try to solve many problems without sufficient inertia/resources to maintain it all
- don't do enough: just another Linux distro with an added layer to

discover and install apps

- make opinionated tech choices I don't agree with
- have a limited list of apps in their app stores and exclude the ones I want
- have too many apps in their app store, without good ways to compare quality, privacy, features
- are GUI (graphical user interface)-focused where I prefer working on a command line

Still, check 'em out. They might work better for you if you don't need the level of power and control provided by this book. By the time I publish, they (or some new contenders) might grow to overcome my approach. Please let me know what you discover. If I missed something, I'd love to learn about it!

Here are some more related and interesting self-hosting solutions worth researching further:

- Ansible NAS [https://github.com/davestephens/ansible-nas]
- Clace [https://clace.io]
- Cosmos Cloud [https://cosmos-cloud.io]
- DockSTARTer [https://dockstarter.com]
- HomelabOS [https://homelabos.com]
- Start9 [https://start9.com]
- MicroCloud [https://canonical.com/microcloud]
- LibreServer [https://libreserver.org]
- LinuxServer.io [https://www.linuxserver.io]
- NextcloudPi [https://nextcloudpi.com]
- UBOS [https://ubos.net]

12. Discussion topics

Here are some conversation starters for a class or small group.

1. What services do *you* run? Why? For whom?
2. What are some considerations when choosing between public cloud and on-premise self-hosting?
3. Compare and contrast different options for bare metal self-hosting hardware in terms of setup cost, power usage, and expandability.
4. Why does the author encrypt all network traffic, even in a closed LAN?
5. Review this book for poor security practices. How might it be improved?
6. Why is privacy important, especially with digital information?
7. What's the best part about self-hosting?
8. What are some pitfalls of self-hosting?
9. What is the future of self-hosting?
10. What is the ideal number of users to support with a single self-hosted server?
11. Is the *Steadfast* method useful for larger groups, big families,

church congregations, schools, businesses, and governements? Why or why not?

12. How might this book be adapted for:

    a. intermittent power

    b. intermittent network

    c. local-only network

    d. clustered hardware

13. Consider FOSS with respect to human attention and focus. Contrast with non-FOSS.

14. What approaches in this book may be conceptually dangerous or misleading? Why? How could they be improved?

15. Summarize this book in one sentence.

16. How might you detect if your server has been compromised?

13. Exercises

Exercises for individual practice and study groups.

1. Stand up a service besides those included with mario using an existing image. For example, a `dashboard` [https://awesome-selfhosted.net/tags/personal-dashboards.html].
2. Build a custom image. Hint: use `docker build` or `Buildah` [https://buildah.io].
3. Run a container using your custom image.
4. Create a service (using your container) to know if it is time to reboot your server. Hint: check if `/host/var/run/reboot-required` exists.
5. Stand up a second Nextcloud service for experiments. Use it to test out the latest release or a custom app.
6. Try Nextcloud with object storage for primary storage.
7. Adapt this guide to a Linux distribution besides Ubuntu.
8. Help resolve a bug mentioned in this book.
9. Set up periodic automatic offsite backups.
10. Add a GPU to your server.

11. Enable GPU transcoding in Jellyfin.

12. Sign the open letter at Public Money, Public Code [https://publiccode.eu] because software paid for with taxes should be FOSS.

13. Aggregate logs.

14. Pick a Docker container that doesn't need to be able to initiate outbound network connections. Prevent it from doing so and prove to yourself it works.

15. What if the server won't boot?

    a. Describe troubleshooting steps, in detail.

    b. Make a plan for system recovery when it fails to boot.

16. Set up single sign-on [https://en.wikipedia.org/wiki/Single_sign-on].

17. Set up Fail2Ban [https://fail2ban.org]. Feed it logs from various services.

18. Set up Suricata [https://suricata.io] network analysis and threat detection.

19. Try running containers with podman [https://podman.io].

20. Read up on other ways to isolate processes, e.g. FreeBSD jails and chroot.

21. Contribute to mario.

22. Move secrets used by mario into an Ansible vault or a self-hosted service intended for managing secrets.

23. Adapt mario to use podman.

24. Adapt mario to use Kubernetes [https://kubernetes.io].

25. If you have a dynamic WAN IP address, create or use an existing dynamic DNS update client container.

26. Stand up a mail relay container such as github.com/crazy-max/docker-msmtpd or github.com/namshi/docker-smtp. Allow all mario-managed services to send email through this relay.

27. Stand up your own DNS server.

28. Reorganize mario services into distinct Ansible roles. Upload the roles to Ansible Galaxy [https://galaxy.ansible.com] as a playbook bundle.

29. Traefik's Docker integration has security implications [https://doc.traefik.io/traefik/providers/docker/#docker-api-access]. Test these risks against your security considerations following Section 6.2.3, "Threat model". If you should mitigate this risk based on your threat model, harden mario so even if Traefik were compromised it would not compromise the whole server. Review the Traefik docs on this topic and tearfik-hardened [https://github.com/wollomatic/traefik-hardened] to get some ideas.

30. Modify mario to always run containers as unprivileged (non-root) users [https://docs.docker.com/engine/security/userns-remap/].

31. Use appropriate ownership and permissions for persistent container data.

32. Set up Nextcloud Talk high-performance backend [https://github.com/strukturag/nextcloud-spreed-signaling#running-with-docker].

33. Uncomplicated Firewall and Docker do not get along well [https://docs.docker.com/network/packet-filtering-firewalls/#docker-and-ufw]. Work around this and share your solution with others.

34. Try Nix and NixOS [https://nixos.org].

35. Roll your own Linux distro.

36. Build, configure and deploy an OPNsense firewall [https://opnsense.org].

37. Set up your own headscale [https://headscale.net] VPN/tailnet for remote LAN access.

38. Improve preview/thumbnail generation in Nextcloud.

    a. Research first: Will you and your users benefit from the change? Are there security implications? How does default preview generation work? What file types are supported by the default previewer and other previewers? How much disk space is used? How fast is it, subjectively and objectively? What maintenance will it require once enabled?

b. Create a test bed with a clean install and many preview-able files of various file formats. Find or write code for recording objective performance metrics (e.g. time it takes to generate previews for a folder containing many files of various types). Consider both client- and server-side performance. Keep manual testing notes (subjective measurements).

c. Compare Preview Generator [https://apps.nextcloud.com/apps/previewgenerator], Imaginary [https://github.com/h2non/imaginary], and any other extant previewers.

d. Establish baseline performance metrics before making any changes.

e. Enable one or the other, get timings, repeat for each previewer.

f. Evaluate the change. Is it noticeable? Does your timing script show any difference? How much disk space is used for previews? How challenging was this to enable?

The detailed steps in the last exercise suggest what may be required in general to achieve better outcomes. I've omitted them from the other exercises for brevity. Please apply similar detailed steps elsewhere as desired.

Afterword

In the words of Scott McNealy, former CEO of Sun Microsystems:

> Open source is free like a puppy is free.

Everybody loves a puppy, right? *Right??* I sure hope so. Because—fair warning—if you spend too much time with your "puppy" (self-hosting, FOSS, etc.), your partner will show up with an actual puppy.

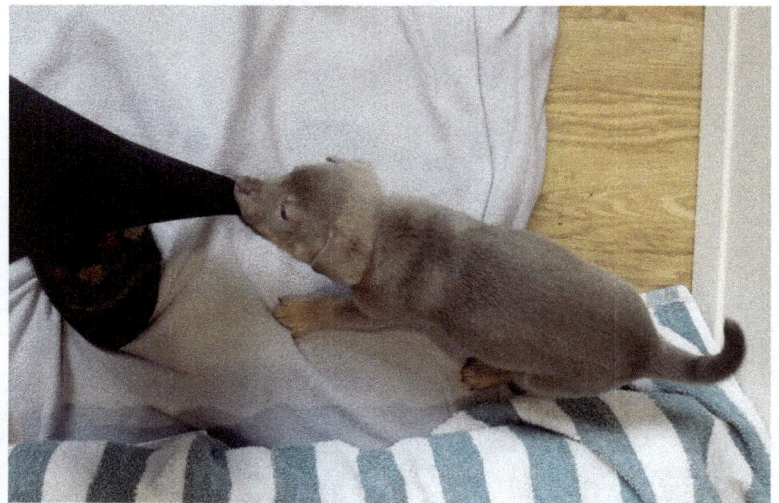

Figure 17. Open Source is free like a puppy. Pictured: actual puppy.

If your problem is *that* cute, I suppose it's not too a bad problem to have. I hope you find what you need to keep *your* puppies happy!

Finally, I'd like to share an Ursula K. Le Guin quote. According to her:

> A book is just a box of words until a reader opens it.

Dear Reader, *this book exists because you exist*. I hope it serves you well. I am humbled and grateful for your support. Thank you, thank you, thank you.

Acknowledgments

Sometimes I feel more like a birthday boy than an author, accepting gifts from so many generous people. I truly couldn't have done this alone and I am so, so grateful for you.

Thanks to Eva for more than I could ever account for here, from "What if it rains?" to leading by learning and fearlessly doing. For supporting my dreams, including this book: your several inspiring rounds of thoughtful code review, technical critique, developmental editing, copy editing, proof reading, and line editing.

Thanks to my daughter for your fantastic illustrations.

Thanks to Deb Nicholson for writing the meaningful Foreword.

Thanks to my family and friends for tolerating my protracted FOSS self-hosting boondoggles, including this book.

Thanks to *Pro Git 2*, my inspiration to switch to Asciidoctor.

Thanks to the contributors to the myriad FOSS programs I used to create this book, especially John MacFarlane and the Pandoc team, Dan Allen and the Asciidoctor team, and Bram Moolenaar and the Vim team (rest in peace, Bram).

Thanks to Rob Smith and all #underlug for help with hardware, networking, Ansible, and Traefik.

Thanks to the "Deadbeat Dads" Bryan Daisley and Rob Floberg for your invaluable feedback.

Thanks to all my beloved beta testers, including Andrew Davidson, Brendan Kidwell, Eva Monsen, Don O'Neill, and Lenny Wondra.

Thanks to Bob Nystrom for your mind-expanding design review.

Thanks to Lenny Wondra for your deeply effective tech review and editing.

Thanks most of all to my wife and kids for supporting and believing in me. For all the cooking, talking, listening, art, coding, math, music, and love. Aren't we lucky?!

Glossary

Here's a list of definitions for some of the more non-obvious terms I use in this book to clarify how I use them. These stick to common use as much as possible. Specialists in computer science, security, administration, networking and so on will have more nuanced definitions.

AI

Artificial intelligence.

API

Application programming interface. Provides a way to interact with a service from software. Useful for writing apps and integrations.

attack surface

Total of possible attack vectors. Fewer is more secure. Example: closing all but the ports you need open reduces yours.

backend

I use this term to refer to either a service (e.g. a database) or server. It's something you more frequently interact with indirectly, say, via a frontend like a web app or mobile UI.

bare metal

Physical nearby computing resources, as opposed to rented compute time on someone else's hardware. Used in this book primarily to indicate hardware autonomy.

block storage

Cloud storage option with direct filesystem access including files and folders. Used directly/natively/locally from an OS. Size is relatively fixed and determined at creation time.

bot

Short for robot. Software performing autonomous tasks such as responding to chat requests or attacking vulnerable servers.

cattle vs. pets

Highlights two distinct sysadmin approaches to systems/services. Cattle are automated, ephemeral, and hopefully immutable. Pets are managed manually, stateful, and long-lived.

cert

Shorthand for HTTPS encryption certificate.

change management

The means and methods of transitioning a group of people from one set of tools and processes to another.

cloud

An ambiguous amount of remote hardware. Scalable, programmable, and networked. "The cloud" or "public cloud" is someone else's hardware while "personal cloud" is your own.

cluster

Collated collection of machines treated as a single machine to achieve higher scale computing power.

compute

Noun: CPU or GPU resources expended when running software services.

container

Running instance of an image. Containers may also be referred to as "guests", although this is more commonly used to describe VMs.

CPU

Central processing unit. The main brain of the computer; the place where most of the math happens.

data

Noun, plural. Yes, I use the annoying plural form! Sorry, old habit.

data sovereignty

Full control of your data. For example, having original copies of your files.

deploy

Prepare a service for use. Typically involves building or copying files before a service is started.

dogfooding

Being a user of something you also created and/or maintain. "Eat your own dogfood."

DHCP

Dynamic Host Configuration Protocol. This is one way computers get IP addresses and related networking settings.

DIY

Do it yourself. Said of activities involving some amount of learning and tinkering you'd otherwise pay for. Cooking, for example. Also: self-hosting.

DNS

Domain Name System. Maps domain names to IP addresses.

domain name

How a server, service, or group of services are identified, e.g. `example.com`.

DRM

Digital restrictions management. Ancient, evil technology designed to prevent unapproved consumption of content. Probably used for surveillance too.

egress

Any outbound data transfer or download, in public cloud terms.

entrypoint

How traffic enters the Traefik reverse proxy; network ports.

firewall

Means of controlling network traffic between computers.

fork

Verb: to split one software project into two. Noun: a derivative software work. The fork diverges from the original (otherwise it would simply be a copy). One or many software projects may succeed the original. Forking software is a useful and common activity.

FOSS

Free and open-source software. An acronym designed to unite the goals of the FSF and the OSI.

FSF

Free Software Foundation. They strongly defend the "F" in FOSS.

frontend

The UI for a system or service.

full-disk encryption

When an entire storage area is cryptographically protected.

GB

Gigabyte. $1,000^3$ (1,000,000,000) bytes for HDDs, or $1,024^3$ (1,073,741,824) bytes for RAM.

good, fast, and cheap

Used with a wink in this text because typically we must pick two [https://en.wikipedia.org/wiki/Project_management_triangle].

Good Thing

A hand-wavy way of saying something is self-evidently wonderful.

groupware

Software for group collaboration. Loosely: mail, calendar, and contacts. Sometimes includes collborative editing of office documents and spreadsheets.

GPU

Graphics processing unit. Originally intended for graphics. Found to be useful for many specialized compute workloads including transcoding video.

GUI

Graphical user interface.

HDD

Hard disk drive. Stores ones and zeros on spinning metal platters.

homelab

A physical or conceptional space for do-it-yourself flexible systems administration leaning and experimentation. A homelab is not quite what this book describes, it is more of an at-home hardware, software, and electronics maker-space. A *Steadfast* server (or "personal cloud") should be nearly always online and useful—at least the user-facing part. Some self-hosters call this environment "homeprod". Far from this level of hair-splitting detail, I'll use "homelab" as a shortcut for "self-hosting setup" and/or "homeprod".

host

The computer where Docker containers run. Also called a "server" in this text.

hostname

Name for a single server/computer/device.

HVAC

Heating, ventilation, and air conditioning.

idempotent

An operation which enacts changes only until an end state is reached. Repeating the operation has no effect once the end state is reached. For example, updating an OS. After the OS is up to date, updating again will cause no changes to the list of installed packages (assuming no new updates become available while updating).

image

A filesystem with code and dependencies necessary to run a container.

immutable

Doesn't change. For example, a particular Docker image. A container instantiated from that image can be modified, but the image cannot; a new image must be built.

IPMI

Intelligent Platform Management Interface. Used for remote server management including reboots and OS installs.

IPS

Intrusion prevention system. Mitigates the risk of penetration.

isolation

For software services: Keep separate from others. Eases sysadmin tasks such as preventing dependency version conflicts.

ISP

Internet service provider.

kernel

The part of the OS that talks directly with hardware.

LAN

Local area network. For example, the network used by computers and devices to talk with each other inside your home.

LFNW

LinuxFest Northwest. Annual conference in Bellingham, Washington dedicated to serving and connecting open source communities. Established in 2000.

Linux

The most popular server OS. Also works fine on a desktop or laptop. The old me would have insisted on calling it "GNU/Linux" or "a Linux distribution". A lot has happened since then, and I've come to believe "Linux" is enough to describe the OS used for self-hosting in the context of this book.

low-code

High-level application development platform with reduced focus on traditional programming. Typically provides a GUI and requires less files with configuration and code. Useful for prototyping or replacing some simpler data entry and analysis applications.

LTS

Long-term support. A stable software release, supported for many years.

mario

Provisioning system included with this book to assist with learning how to set up and maintain your own server. Consists of scripts, documentation, and configuration files.

NAS

Network-attached storage. A server made for storing data. Usually has several HDD bays in a non-rackmount box-like form factor. Likely has less CPU and RAM (and less power usage) than what I describe in Section 7.2.1, "Server".

NIC

Network interface card, also called a network adapter. Hardware for receiving and sending data over a network.

object storage

Relatively unlimited and typically remote cloud storage option. Actual data are abstracted: backups and structured access require special services, indexes, and software.

OCR

Optical character recognition. The process of converting images of text to actual text.

OOB

Out-of-band (management). A means of remote low-level server control including power cycling and console interaction, typically provided by an independently powered and networked embedded computer. See also: IPMI.

OS

Operating system.

OSI

Open Source Initiative. More concerned with the "OSS" of FOSS.

PHP

PHP: Hypertext Processor. Programming language built for the web.

PoE

Power over ethernet. Utilizes an ethernet cable for electricity as well as data.

port

Along with an IP address, a number used to connect to a service. Reserved port numbers such as 80 for HTTP are listed in `/etc/services`.

partition

Delineated section of a HDD or block storage, formatted with a filesystem such as ext4 or ZFS.

port forward

Router configuration to send traffic for a particular port to a computer inside a LAN.

process

Instance of running software. Note that "running" processes are described in more detail by a lower-level state such as running, sleeping, idle, waiting for I/O completion and—my personal favorite—zombie.

provision

As in, "provision a server". Set up a machine or otherwise bring it into alignment with a known/good configuration.

RAID

Redundant array of inexpensive disks. Allows flexible use of multiple drives for redundancy and/or speed, as desired.

reproducible

Able to be repeated following specific steps. E.g. "repro" a bug or "a reproducible [software] build". If two people try to repro a bug, they should have the same experience. If two people each build an image from the same `Dockerfile`, they should produce the same image. In practice, bug repros and build products are close enough and never exactly the same.

reverse proxy

Networking software for filtering and directing traffic. In a self-hosted context, useful for SSL termination and for running several self-hosted web services with different domain names with a single IP address.

router

Network device used to handle traffic at the boundary between networks such as a WAN and LAN. A SOHO router typically also provides various other functions including DNS, DHCP, switching, firewalling, and Wi-Fi. See: port forward. A Traefik router is something different: this is a software logic connecting entrypoints to services. See Section 6.6.1, "Traefik architecture".

runtime

The period of time when a software is running; when a set of machine instructions becomes a running process. Also used to describe a set of tools/libraries to facilitate same. May appear as "runtime environment" in the latter form.

SeaGL

Seattle GNU/Linux Conference. Held yearly since 2013.

server

A computer that generally stays powered on and uses networking for interaction instead of a monitor, keyboard, or mouse. Also called a "host".

service

A long-running process used by other local and remote processes to do something useful.

SOHO

Small office / home office.

source control

A system for tracking changes in source code along with who made the change, why, and when. Git is one such system.

source of truth

The authoritative (home for a) document, perhaps among some number of available choices/copies.

SSD

Solid-state drive. A hard drive that doesn't spin.

SSH

Secure Shell. Provides encrypted remote command line access to a server.

SSL termination

Accepting encrypted traffic and passing along unencrypted traffic. Act performed by Traefik reverse proxy in a mario-provisioned server. More accurately and less often referred to as "TLS termination". Actual SSL is deprecated.

sysadmin

Portmanteau of "systems administrator". A party responsible for the upkeep of a computer system.

threat model

Analysis of risks and defenses of digital assets.

TB

Terabyte. Like GB, can be either base-10 or base-2, so: $1,000^4$ (1,000,000,000,000) bytes for HDDs and $1,024^4$ (1,099,511,627,776) bytes for RAM.

TLD

Top-level domain. For "example.com", ".com" is the TLD.

UI

User interface. The means of interaction between a user and a system, e.g.: a web site or mobile app. Often considered along with user experience and notated "UI/UX".

UPS

Uninterruptible power supply. A battery that sits between your server and an outlet, often with extra features such as a power outage alarm or surge suppressor.

UX

User experience. The nature of interaction between a user and a system they are using. Includes ease of use and steps involved to complete a task. Often considered along with user interface and written as "UI/UX".

volume

> Docker facility to mount a folder on the server to a folder inside a container. This is a common means of persisting container data that would otherwise be ephemeral.

VM

> Virtual machine. OS isolation technique simulating nearly all aspects of hardware including power, input, and output.

VPN

> Virtual private network. Useful to "teleport home" and behave (from a networking perspective) as if you are inside your home LAN.

WAN

> Wide-area network. Everything outside your LAN / home network / router.

ZFS

> A filesystem with many advanced features such as encryption, bit rot mitigation, journaling, volume management, and snapshotting. Used to stand for Zettabyte File System.

Index

A

admin computer, 62, 74, 77
AI, 60, 102, 139
Ansible, 73, 128
API, 86, 139
attack surface, 46, 127, 139

B

backend, 139
backups, 27, 71
    using Borg for, 71
    using restic for, 71
bare metal, 6, 14, 17, 33, 140
block storage, 63, 140
Borg, 71
bot, 45, 140

C

CasaOS, 126
cattle vs. pets, 52, 140
cert, 84, 140
change management, 39, 140
Clace, 128
cloud, 6, 15, 21, 140
cluster, 50, 140
Collabora, 118
compute, 17, 60, 140
container, 33, 48, 51, 141
Cosmos Cloud, 128
CPU, 141

D

data, 141
data sovereignty, 5, 14-15, 63, 141
deploy, 141
DHCP, 141
DIY, 126, 141
DNS, 78, 103, 141
Docker, 33, 50
Docker Compose, 51, 56, 70, 126
DockSTARTer, 128
dogfooding, 35, 62, 141
domain name, 141

DRM, 142

E

egress, 63, 142
encryption
    full-disk, 46
    HTTPS, 84
entrypoint, 53, 142
ext4, 48

F

firewall, 64, 142
fork, 57, 142
FOSS, 21, 102, 142
    author's bias towards, 21
FreedomBox, 126
frontend, 142
FSF, 142
full-disk encryption, 142

G

GB, 142
Good Thing, 143
good, fast, and cheap, 143
GPU, 102, 143
groupware, 117-118, 143
GUI, 143

H

HDD, 63, 143
homelab, 143
HomelabOS, 128
host, 143
hostname, 144
HTTPS, 53, 84
HVAC, 27, 144

I

idempotent, 74, 144
image, 51, 144
immutable, 144
IPMI, 61, 65, 144
IPS, 45, 144
isolation, 34, 51, 144
ISP, 64, 144

J

Jellyfin, 34, 91
    using a GPU with, 91
Jitsi, 35

K

kernel, 144
Kubernetes, 50

L

LAN, 6, 45-46, 64, 80, 145
Let's Encrypt, 84
LFNW, 1, 145
LibreServer, 128
Linux, 49, 145
LinuxServer.io, 128
low-code, 115, 145
LTS, 49, 145

M

maintenance
    server, 68
mario, 73, 145
MicroCloud, 128
middleware, 103, 106-107

N

NAS, 126, 145

Nextcloud, 57, 89
    apps for, 111
    full text search and, 116
    installing, 107, 123
    mobile and, 116, 119
    office and, 118
    ownCloud vs., 118
    release cadence of, 110
    security and, 107
    surprises with, 35
NextcloudPi, 128
NIC, 146

O

object storage, 63, 107, 146
OCR, 34, 146
ONLYOFFICE, 118
OOB, 146
OpenSSH, 75
operating system, 49, 146
OSI, 146
ownCloud, 58, 118

P

Pandoc, 20
Paperless-ngx, 34
partition, 146
password manager, 43
PHP, 146
Pi-hole, 103
Plex, 34
PoE, 146
port, 146
port forward, 44, 147
process, 147
prosocial behavior, 5

provision, 74, 147

R

RAID, 48, 63, 147
reproducible, 52, 147
restic, 71
reverse proxy, 52, 82, 147
router, 6, 44, 64, 147
    Traefik, 53
runtime, 148
Runtipi, 126

S

Scratch, 98
SeaGL, 2, 102, 148
server, 148
service, 148
Single sign-on, 105
SOHO, 16, 148
source control, 148
source of truth, 15, 148
SSD, 63, 148
SSH, 6, 49, 105, 148
SSL termination, 84, 149
Start9, 128
sysadmin, 149
    mindset of a Steadfast, 39

T

TB, 149
threat model, 44, 149
TLD, 149
Traefik, 34, 53, 82

U

UBOS, 128
Ubuntu, 49

UI, 149
UPS, 149
UX, 149

V

Vim, 20
VM, 33, 50, 150
volume, 150
VPN, 46, 150

W

Wallabag, 94
WAN, 150
WAN access, 44-45, 106
Watchtower, 70, 96
Wireguard, 46

Y

YunoHost, 126

Z

ZFS, 48, 150
    setting up, 66
    snapshots and, 63, 70

www.ingramcontent.com/pod-product-compliance
Lightning Source LLC
Chambersburg PA
CBHW060837190426
43197CB00040B/2658